THE CONSTITUTION

AND WHAT IT MEANS

WILLIAM JAMES

iUniverse, Inc.
Bloomington

The Constitution and What It Means

iUniverse books may be ordered through booksellers or by contacting:

iUniverse
1663 Liberty Drive
Bloomington, IN 47403
www.iuniverse.com
1-800-Authors (1-800-288-4677)

Because of the dynamic nature of the Internet, any web addresses or links contained in this book may have changed since publication and may no longer be valid. The views expressed in this work are solely those of the author and do not necessarily reflect the views of the publisher, and the publisher hereby disclaims any responsibility for them.

Any people depicted in stock imagery provided by Thinkstock are models, and such images are being used for illustrative purposes only.

Certain stock imagery © Thinkstock.

ISBN: 978-1-4759-3464-9 (sc)
ISBN: 978-1-4759-3465-6 (e)
ISBN: 978-1-4759-3466-3 (hc)

Library of Congress Control Number: 2012912193

Printed in the United States of America

iUniverse rev. date: 07/27/2012

"The American People won't make a mistake if they are given all the facts"

Thomas Jefferson

"Whensoever the General Government assumes undelegated powers, its acts are unauthoritative, void, and of no force."

Thomas Jeffeerson

Contents

A
CHRONOLOGY

July 4, 1776	Declaration of Independence
May 25, 1787	Constitutional Congress Convenes
September 17, 1787	Congress adopts the Constitution sends it to the states for ratification.
December 7, 1787	Delaware becomes the first state to ratify the constitution.
December 12, 1787	Pennsylvania ratifies.
December 18, 1787	New Jersey ratifies.
January 9, 1788	Georgia ratifies.
January 9, 1788	Connecticut ratifies.
February 6, 1788	Massachusetts ratifies.
April 28, 1788	Maryland ratifies.
May 23, 1788	South Carolina ratifies.
June 21, 1788	New Hampshire – the ninth state to ratify the Constitution making it the Supreme law of the land.
June 25, 1788	Virginia ratifies.
July 26, 1788	New York ratifies
March 4, 1789	The Constitution goes into effect.
November 21, 1789	North Carolina ratifies.

| May 29, 1790 | Rhode Island ratifies. |
| December 15, 1791 | Virginia becomes the eleventh state to ratify the Bill of Rights thereby incorporating them into the Constitution. |

CHAPTER 1

For far too long the Constitution has been viewed as a complex, almost mystical document. The ensuing pages will remove the shroud of mystery surrounding it, that our Congress men and women have perpetuated. We will expose the man behind the curtain, called Congress, and let him know we figured it out. He works for us, not the other way around. We will take our lead from the recognized father of the Constitution, James Madison in Federalists[1] number thirty-seven when he said, "The ultimate object of these papers is to determine clearly and fully the merits of this Constitution."

Before we can accomplish our goal we must have the courage to face the truth and let reason be our guide. For example, if you believe in manmade Global Warming, you will not believe this book; for reason does not have a prominent role in your thought process. If you hate America, you will despise this book. If Al Gore is your mentor, James Madison is your

---

[1] James Madison, Alexander Hamilton and John Jay wrote the Federalist Papers; a series of eighty five papers published during the ratification process to explain the Constitution.

nemeses. "Every man has a right to his own opinions, but no man has a right to be wrong in facts,"[2]

Throughout the history of mankind governments have sought to control its people. For centuries that control has been accomplished through fear. Today our congressmen, unfortunately, are no different. However, our Constitution makes that control somewhat problematic. On the other hand they have hit upon one of the greatest hoaxes of all time.[3] They have led us down the path to the altar of global warming. If we don't sacrifice everything at this altar we will all surely die. The Constitution 'be damned,' give me your freedom, your liberty and your money for only then can you be saved. Politicians who preach at the altar of global-warming are creating the chloroform that makes the separation of man from, his money, liberty and freedom a lot more palatable. Anyone foolish enough to follow them over this cliff will have a mortal fear of a Constitution that when fully understood requires one to be a self-reliant, rugged, individual.

Although, the words Self-reliant, rugged, individual do not appear in the Constitution it becomes manifestly clear in the Declaration of Independence with the often quoted passage to "...pursue life, liberty and happiness..." that everyone is an individual who is the sole arbiter of what will make them happy and that happiness is determined by self-reliant, rugged, individualism. Our Constitution enshrines the concept of property rights through self-reliant, rugged, individualism. The founding fathers did not have social security, Medicare, healthcare or any form of government welfare. They were

---

[2] Bernard Baruch, American Economist 1870 - 1965
[3] Trickle Down Tyranny,The Myth of Global Warming, Chapter 9, Michael Savage.

2

completely vested in the concept of self-reliant, rugged, individualism. To be sure, the founders were generous with their wealth but it was always an individual choice, not a government mandate. The very last sentence of The Declaration of Independence sums up the entire concept of self-reliant, rugged, individualism where those who signed their names to that document said, "...we mutually pledge to each other our Lives, our Fortunes and our sacred Honor." Today's congress has taken away our self-reliant, rugged, individualism and taxed our Lives, Fortunes and Honor.

The federal government was designed to play only a small role. As a matter of fact the federal government was so small its twenty one duties were listed in Article I, section 8, however, as we shall soon see only the legal profession demonstrated the incompetence to fully misunderstand the simplicity of the US Constitution.

To fully understand the simplicity of our Constitution we must first understand that the legal profession, both lawyers and judges are also human; like the rest of us they are subject to the weaknesses of human nature in that they too are not infallible. It has been noted that the only requirements to be a judge are (1) obtain a law degree (2) be appointed by the president and (3) be confirmed by the Senate. It is the job of the federal judiciary to focus on the constitutionality of our laws, nothing more, and nothing less. A judge that cannot separate his or her personal beliefs from the true meaning of the Constitution is a dangerous tyrant. In 2012 Ruth Bader Ginsberg while offering advice to the newly formed Egyptian Muslim Brotherhood stated she would not look to the US Constitution for guidance. A Supreme Court Justice, who took an oath to defend and protect the Constitution, advises a foreign nation on foreign soil not to look toward the U.S. Constitution- a truly impeachable offense, if ever there was one, and not so much as a single eye brow was raised in Congress.

The federal judiciary, legislature or executive also have no constitutional authority to regulate our economy. Historians have exposed the disaster of government involvement in economics. More specifically, many historians today have detailed the overwhelming negative consequences of Franklin Roosevelt's New Deal; a policy that not only prolonged but exacerbated the Great Depression. The New Deal was unconstitutional.

Whenever you see the word unconstitutional, it is a euphuism for supremely illegal. The Constitution is the Supreme law of the land. When our congress men and women pass unconstitutional laws, they are not simply breaking the law; they are breaking the Supreme law of the land. In other words, the petty thief is not as nearly corrupt as the well dressed Congress Man or Woman who abdicates their Constitutional responsibility.

A good leader will learn from history. However, we see our 21st century leaders making the same mistakes of the past; such actions not only demonstrate the bold ignorance of today's leaders but also expose the complete vapidness of higher education. It is the responsibility of the institutions of higher learning to teach history. More often than not our leaders come from the Ivy League schools, a clear sign for parents to steer clear of Ivy League educations for their children. It not only appears to dumb down the individual, but it wastes hundreds of thousands of dollars in tuition fees while creating a terribly weak leadership class. Perhaps the late William F. Buckley Jr. was on to something when he said, "I would rather be governed by the first two thousand people in the Manhattan phone book, than the entire faculty of Harvard."[4] Thomas Sowell is even more succinct when he said, "Academic pedigree is no grantor of useful knowledge."

Today we have a federal government (my congressman and yours) who are proudly proclaiming only they can save the economy and save the country. That is wrong on so many levels it would require another book. Suffice it to say, our congressmen are clearly driven by socialism not the tenants of the United States Constitution. It is probably all we can expect from people who tout the failed policies of the past and scorn the success of our founders. In other words let us heed the warning of Justice Robert H. Jackson when he wrote of himself and his fellow justices, "We are not final because we are infallible, but we are infallible only because we are final." This book lays bare the true meaning of our Constitution.

To fully understand the Constitution we must first disabuse ourselves of the notion that only the legal profession is qualified to explain it. The recognized father of our Constitution, James Madison, was not a lawyer. As you will soon learn it was the legal profession that created the problems with our Constitution, not solve them. John Lescroart in his novel *Guilt* captures the essence of the legal profession when he says, "I am a lawyer...first we argue, then we deflect the direction words might be going to win, we...obfuscate." The Constitution is not a difficult document, unless of course, you are a lawyer. Just because someone speaks with an air of authority doesn't make it so. Even Thomas Jefferson recognized the minimal ability of lawyers more than two hundred years ago when he said, "If

---

[4] Book, William F. Buckley Jr. Quotes

the present Congress err in too much talking, how can it be otherwise in a body to which the people send one hundred and fifty lawyers, whose trade it is to question everything, yield nothing, and talk by the hour?"

It is not the job of a lawyer to find the truth it is only, instead, to create doubt, especially about our Constitution. We will remove that doubt. The very linchpin of the legal profession is that a defendant must be found guilty beyond all reasonable doubt. All a lawyer need do then is create doubt in the mind of a single juror. The most famous case to date is the OJ Simpson murder trial. The quote by Thomas Jefferson is as poignant today as when it was written; a lawyer yields nothing, talks by the hour and creates doubt. Asking a lawyer to explain the Constitution is like asking a plumber to perform a heart by-pass. We need not turn to a lawyer for the definition to our Constitution; but instead we take our lead from Hamilton when he says, "The rules of legal interpretation are rules of common sense." Probably the single greatest characteristic the legal profession lacks.

It is the nature of the American people to respect authority. The confines of a court room are by its very nature authoritative and imposing. The court room creates an environment of awe and respect. Lawyers are trained to manipulate these circumstances to their advantage. After all, when the oracle speaks everyone listens. The 110th Congress which ended December 2008 had 179 lawyers in the House and 56 Senators who held law degrees. The public favorability rating hit an all time low at 14%.[5] Clearly this is not a segment of the population held in high esteem. How is it then, these same people continue to be reelected? It has been said that all politics

---

[5] November 17, 2008 Gallup poll

are local politics. The American people are a trusting group, when we meet, for example, a Hillary Clinton, Barney Frank, Nancy Pelosi or Harry Reid, one on one, they are gracious, polite, well spoken always nice and invariably tell us what we want to hear. We leave the encounter with the idea that it is everyone else's Senator who are the corrupt ones, when in fact it is we who just got conned. Remember Thomas Jefferson's admonition they, "...yield nothing and talk by the hour." Perhaps it is a redundancy to say they also know nothing about the Constitution for if they did, government (our congressmen) would be the well behaved child in the crowd who was seen but not heard. After all it is an important and demanding position; not to worry, we think the Constitution will keep restraints on their activity, as we shall see it does not. When we meet our personal Congressman we are always overwhelmed by his knowledge and compassion. Yes we all agree Congress as a group is poor, but invariably we all seem to fall into the trap that it isn't our Congressman who is the problem.

The arrogance of a lawyers has always amazed me. When elected to office they automatically view themselves as economist, and begin to attack the economy as though it were some defendant in court. On the other hand, when economists are elected to office they are humble enough to realize they are not lawyers. If you are charged with a serious crime, who will you turn to for help, the economist or the lawyer? Likewise, why do we turn to a lawyer for direction on our economy, or the Constitution for that matter? The lawyer is trained to speak in language that sounds impressive and authoritative but as John Lescroart has demonstrated it is only to "...obfuscate." A lawyer is no economist. Likewise, a lawyer is no constitutional scholar, therefore, let us not turn our economy or our Constitution over to a group of lawyers who's only contribution according to Jefferson is to "…yield nothing and talk by the hour."

Also, contrary to popular belief the Constitution, although, the supreme law of the land is not written in 'legalese,' as our congressmen would have us believe. The language is certainly flowery, but consistent with the spoken language of the day. In order for it to be accepted by the States it had to be understood by everyone. Furthermore, let us not forget a high school education in the 18th century was equivalent to today's bachelor's degree.

Every economist clearly understands he is no lawyer, but every lawyer thinks he is an economist, an attorney, and a Constitutional scholar. A few such examples: Harry Reid, Hillary Clinton, Ted Kennedy, Barney Frank, John Kerry are all economic charlatans. The last three from the state of Massachusetts – God help them. With arrogance like that, no wonder they are trampling our Constitution. "Legal training should not be confused with an education."[6]

The Constitution was born out of American exceptionalism, something so unique it had never been tried. An experiment so profound it drew nothing from past dynasties except the understanding they were not the proper path for this new land called America. This bold new experience came to be known as conservatism. An ideology that manifest itself in a free market economy with a small limited government that allowed the self reliant, rugged, individualism we call the American spirit to flourish. People would come from all over the world to a place called America, because here you would be left alone by government. People came here not to change each other but to

[6] Kevin R.C. Gutzman, *The Politically Incorrect guide to the Constitution*

change themselves through self reliant, rugged, individualism. It would be those characteristics that defined this new place called America. Its traditions, its religion, and its philosophy were accepted and understood. "e pluribus unum" the motto of our great nation, "From many we unite as one." It would be with this spirit that the new Constitution would be conceived.

This new world would have a Constitution that would protect "life, liberty and the pursuit of happiness." It would guarantee equal rights but not equal outcome. The new world recognized that all men were created equal but not all men would be basketball players, football players, doctors or God forbid more lawyers, some might become Joe the plumber. But, under this new Constitution all men had the equal access to make a choice. A man, if he was so inclined, could choose to do absolutely nothing but it was understood not to be the job of a central government to take from the producers in a society and give to the non producers.

The spirit of our Constitution is captured by Jefferson when he says, "...the government that governs least is the government that governs best." If you turn to the government for all of your solutions, all of your happiness, all of your health care, all of the answers to life's problems you will not find support for these positions in the Constitution. Those ideas are antithetical to the concept of self-reliance, it is not the job of a central government to take money from one and give to someone else. The poor man in your neighborhood, on your street perhaps, is not the responsibility of a central government. That responsibility lies directly with you, the community and that individual.

Today's lawyers in both the government and the courts frequently couch their arguments with the seemingly innocuous statement, "We must look to Europe for guidance." This is not only wrong, it is dangerously wrong. The central purpose of our Constitution was independence from Europe, a clean break from centuries of influence that would have no place in the New World. In a land called America we would take the lead, forage a new direction, and make our own decisions, and never look back only looking forward. As seen in many writings of our forefathers and specifically the Federalists Papers we would only look to Europe to remind us how not to do it. For it now rest with us to determine how it is to be done. We shall look no further than the Constitution of the United States.

The American Constitution was established to embark on a new course; to go forward with a bold new experiment. It would be a new government like history had never seen. The American experience was specifically designed to be unlike anything in the past. This place called American would be that 'shining City on a hill'.[7] It would lead the way with a new system; A system so innovative that one only need look no further than the founding fathers for the true meaning of America. The founding fathers were well steeped in history. As a matter of Fact the Declaration of Independence is a list of some 38 grievances from their immediate past, of which the founders wanted to separate themselves. The entire context of the Federalists Papers reads as though it were a history book. The authors of the Federalist Papers took their lead from the founding fathers who gathered at the Constitutional convention in Philadelphia in 1776. It was necessary to understand the historical inequities so a new government could be crafted to avoid the pitfalls of the past.

---

[7] Reference used by Ronald Regan in his January 1989 Farewell Address.

When a Supreme Court decision, Congress or the Executive Office, for that matter say we must look to Europe for guidance and direction, it not only sets a dangerous precedence it clearly demonstrates complete ignorance by our leaders of our Constitution. Anytime our leaders look beyond the Constitution they are abdicating the very document they have sworn to uphold. Our new government and its Constitution were specifically established to break from the past of Europe or any government on earth for that matter. To fully understand the simplicity and power of the U.S. Constitution and the American experiment is to go no further than our founding fathers. As a matter of fact it bears repeating, the Constitution of the United States is powerful because of its simplicity. ANYONE, ABSOLUTELY ANYONE who says we must look to Europe for guidance is a dangerously arrogant charlatan.

Because the American experiment, as we have learned, was centered on the concept of Self-reliant, rugged, individualism the least a government interferes the greater becomes our potential. We were established to lead the world, not follow. Today's would-be leaders, who choose to follow Europe, are bankrupt of any concept of leadership. It is easy to follow, it takes courage to lead. Lazy, arrogant, incompetent individuals like Joe Biden are antithetical to the concept of self-reliant. He exemplified what it is to be a politician today when he said, "I never had an interest in being a mayor, cause that's a real job, you have to produce."[8] All too frequently, today, the Joe Biden's of the world seek refuge in government office, then want to tell us what is best for us.

In the twenty first century, countries the world over are moving away from socialists forms of government, while our

---

[8] The Examiner March 30, 2012

politicians are moving toward the failed and bankrupt policies of the past. As noted above our Congress is composed of 235 lawyers. This reminds me of another quote from Thomas Jefferson, "Being caught between two lawyers is like a fish out of water, caught between two cats."

The earth is 4.6 billion years old; man has been on earth for only a few thousand of those years. The American experiment is a little more than two hundred years old. However, during those two hundred plus years while the rugged individual was allowed unfettered restraint, we witnessed an explosive growth in life expectancy, health, and the comforts of life. We became the leader in innovation, technology and the entrepreneurial spirit. We have led the world with such inventions as flight, the internal combustion engine, electricity, medicine. While crude oil was being used on a small scale, Whale oil was the dominant source of fuel until we alone unlocked the miracles of crude oil, one of the greatest gifts to mankind. Our contributions to improving the world are so plentiful; they could stand alone in a volume of their own. People come from all over the globe to gain access to our health care while today's politicians want to make our health care like the rest of the world. All these improvements made possible because of our Constitution not our Congressman.

We horde nothing, we share everything thereby making the earth a better place. We have never conquered a single country, a single land or people. We liberate, ask for enough land to bury our dead and return the land to its original owners. We are a benevolent people with a simple desire to succeed, and share our fortunes. Our strength lies in that American experiment established by our founding fathers and that document we call the Constitution. It is a system that rewards the self-reliant, rugged individual who builds a better mouse trap that makes life better for everyone.

Today's political leaders' play on our fears and misunderstanding of the Constitution as well as economics by bashing the rich, but no one has ever received a pay check from a poor man. It has been demonstrated time after time there are only two roads to achievement. The first is to exercise our unalienable right to an unfettered individualism that gives one the freedom to innovate and *serve* his fellow man.

For two hundred years the Great American experience allowed the likes of the Wright Brothers to pursue their invention of flight which benefited all nations. Alexander Graham Bell was not a poor man – he gave us the telephone. Henry Ford was a rags to riches story that gave us the automobile. Sam Walton gained tremendous success but gave us Wal-Mart. Bill Gates, the wealthiest man in the world, gave everyone access to the computer. Our Constitution in its original construction fosters what we call free market capitalism by allowing the individual to pursue his path to individual happiness, from whence the above were able to succeed. Yes, people can become unbelievably wealthy in a free market but there is one underlying thread in all of the above examples. The Constitution fosters accomplishment through self-reliant, rugged, individualism but only when we *serve* our fellow man.

Politicians love to play the greed card. Look at the big oil companies, big pharmaceuticals even Wal-Mart they say. But what is left unsaid – none of those companies would be anywhere without *serving* humanity by producing something we want to purchase. It is not the product that creates success; it is instead, our desire to own the product.

Suppose, for example, Bill Gates was the greediest person on earth, it would make no difference to the consumer because if he did not *serve* his fellow man by producing something we wanted, we simply would not buy it. Now suppose there was another greedy man, we will call him Sidney S. Heartless. Mr. Heartless decides he wants to surpass the wealth of Bill Gates; so he sets about and produces the world's best Widget. Mr. Heartless is so proud of his wonderful high tech Widget that he sets a price so high that if he sells only a few it will make him wealthy beyond all human capacity to comprehend.

People do not want the Widget, it does not sell. Mr. Heartless must lower his price; the Widget still does not sell. Mr. Heartless continues to lower his price until it is below the cost of production but the Widget continues not to sell. The end is obvious; he is bankrupt, out of business and poor. For you see in a free market environment all the greed in the world did not make Mr. Heartless rich. He failed at the single most important principle of free markets; he did not *serve* his fellow man, a concept enshrined by our Constitution.

But wait! There is a second way for Mr. Heartless to get rich. It is, however, the most insipid, most unethical, most destructive and the greatest barrier to success and the entrepreneurial spirit ever envisioned and it is unconstitutional. Government, yes Mr. Heartless need only get his lawyer trained Congressman involved to turn his fortunes around. Of course, that Congressman will get a piece of the action. The political genius, we call our Congressman, will cut his cohorts in on the deal and they will mandate the Widget be produced, after all the Widget, although, expensive will operate on wind and solar power. It will save the universe! Uh Oh, the Widget still does not sell Mr. Heartless and our Congressman still aren't making money on it. No problem, Congress will subsidize the Widget. Mr. Heartless is happy, Congress is happy and Mr. Tax payer is on the hook for yet another Congressional boondoggle. The Constitution supports none of this. As it turns out, it is our Congressman who is the heartless and greedy one, for they have abdicated, once again, their sworn oath to uphold the Constitution and circumvented its constraints by NOT SERVING their fellow man.

As stated at the beginning of this chapter, throughout the history of mankind governments have sought to control its people. Our Constitution severely restricts that control, therefore, it is important that we understand it. Keep reading you will be amazed at how simple it really is.

Chapter 2

Article I

Section 1:

All Legislative Powers herein granted shall be vested in a Congress of the United States which shall consist of a Senate and House of Representatives.

The legislative body, that is, the body responsible for making laws at the federal level will consist of a Congress composed of a Senate and a House of Representatives. Whenever, you see the words "Government," or "Federal Government," remember that is a direct reference to your Congressman and mine. Today that body is 435 members in the House of Representatives and 100 members in the Senate. The first five words, "All Legislative Powers, herein granted...." Is a specific reference as to the powers of Congress being limited to only those defined and identified by the remainder of the Constitution. The following pages are dedicated to identifying those parameters.

Section 2:

The House of Representatives shall be composed of Members chosen every second Year by the People of the several States, and the Electors in each State shall have the Qualifications requisite for Electors of the most numerous Branch of the State Legislature.

Electors here is a reference to you and me, therefore it is we who elect our Representative every two years provided we are citizens of the United States. "The electors are to be the great body of the people of the United States."[9]

No Person shall be a Representative who shall not have attained to the Age of twenty five Years, and been seven Years a Citizen of the United States, and who shall not, when elected, be an Inhabitant of that State in which he shall be chosen.

This clause simply states the qualifications needed for election to the House of Representatives. It is very simple, one only need to be at least twenty five years of age, a resident of the United States for seven years and a resident of the state of which he is seeking election. Now, my and your Representative like to intimidate us into thinking one must have a great deal of experience. Then again the majority of members in Congress are lawyers whose job it is to confuse people. But we will not be confused anymore. Congress was to be a citizen legislature, not a profession

Representatives and direct Taxes shall be apportioned among the several States which may be included within this Union, according to their respective Numbers, which shall be determined by adding to the whole Number of free

---

[9] James Madison Federalists 57

Persons, including those bound to Service for a Term of Years, and excluding Indians not taxed, three fifths of all other Persons.[10]

As this stood before ratification of the Fourteenth Amendment, representation and taxes were determined by population. The Indian population was excluded and each slave was taxed only as three fifths the value of a free person.

The actual Enumeration shall be made within three Years after the first Meeting of the Congress of the United States, and within every subsequent Term of ten Years, in such Manner as they shall by Law direct. The Number of Representatives shall not exceed one for every thirty Thousand, but each State shall have at Least one Representative; and until such enumeration shall be made, the State of New Hampshire shall be entitled to chuse three, Massachusetts eight, Rhode-Island and Providence Plantation one, Connecticut five, New-Your six, New Jersey four, Pennsylvania eight, Delaware one, Maryland six, Virginia ten, North Carolina five, South Carolina five and Georgia three.

Each state is permitted at least one Representative and an additional one for every thirty Thousand in population.[11] Each state must determine by state law how the elections would proceed; however, the elections should take place within three years after the first meeting of Congress. The remainder of the paragraph simply states the number of interim Representatives for each state. This clause also establishes the ten year census. However, all those questions the census takers like to ask, don't have to be answered. The census is to simply count the number

---

[10] Changed by Section 2 of the Fourteenth Amendment

[11] See appendix re: The Fixed History of 435 Representatives

of people for proper representation, anything else is none of their business.

When vacancies happen in the Representation from any State, the Executive Authority thereof shall issue Writs of Election to fill such Vacancies.

Don't be frightened by "Writs of Election" it only means the Governor of a state need only indicate in a formal written document that a special election will be held to fill a vacancy caused by death, imprisonment, impeachment or other reason.

The House of Representatives shall chuse their Speaker and other Officers; "self-explanatory" **and shall have the sole Power of Impeachment.**

The power to impeach arises in the House of Representatives. Once they vote to impeach, as was William Jefferson Clinton on December 19, 1998, then it becomes the responsibility of the Senate to determine if the impeached individual, in this case Clinton, should be removed from office. Although, impeached, the Senate failed to remove him from office.

Section 3:

The Senate of the United States shall be composed of two Senators from each State, (chosen by the Legislature thereof,)[12] **for six Years; and each Senator shall have one Vote.**

This is easy; there will be two Senators from each state with a six year term of office.

Immediately after they shall be assembled in Consequence of the first Election, they shall be divided as equally as may

---

[12] Changed by the Seventeenth Amendment to direct election by the people

be into three Classes. **The Seats of the Senators of the first Class shall be vacated at the Expiration of the second Year, of the second Class at the expiration of the fourth Year, and of the third Class at the Expiration of the sixth Year, so that one third may be chosen every second Year; (and if Vacancies happen by Resignation, or otherwise, during the Recess of the Legislature of any State, the Executive thereof may make temporary Appointments until the next Meeting of the Legislature, which shall then fill such Vacancies.)**[13]

The Senate was divided in such a manner that one third of the seats would be up for election every two years. Until changed by the seventeenth Amendment, the state legislature was responsible for filling vacancies. The executive could only make appointments if the respective state legislature was in recess.

No person shall be a Senator who shall not have attained to the Age of thirty Years, and been nine Years a Citizen of the United States, and who shall not, when elected, be an Inhabitant of that State for which he shall be chosen.

The minimum requirements to be a Senator are to be thirty years of age, at least nine years a citizen of the United States and a resident of the State of which he is chosen. In other words a career politician was not what our forefathers had in mind.

The Vice President of the United States shall be President of the Senate, but shall have no Vote, unless they be equally divided."

The Vice President is President of the Senate and has a vote only when there is a tie.

The Senate shall chuse their other Officers, and also a President pro tempore, in the Absence of the Vice President,

---

[13] Changed by the Seventeenth Amendment

or when he shall exercise the Office of President of the United States.

The Senate alone is responsible for choosing its officers, one of whom must be a President pro tempore, who, in the absence of the Vice President, will take over the duties in the latter's duties in the Senate.

The Senate shall have the sole Power to try all Impeachments. When sitting for the Purpose, they shall be on Oath or Affirmation. When the President of the United States is tried, the Chief Justice shall preside; And no Person shall be convicted without the Concurrence of two thirds of the Members present.

The Senate has sole authority to try all individuals who have been impeached by the House of Representatives, with the Chief Justice of the Supreme Court presiding over Presidential impeachments. A conviction in the Senate must have a two thirds majority of those present.

Judgment in Cases of Impeachment shall not extend further than to removal from Office, and disqualification to hold and enjoy any Office of honor, Trust or Profit under the United States: but the Party convicted shall nevertheless be liable and subject to Indictment, Trial, Judgment and Punishment, according to Law.

If the Senate gathers a two thirds majority after the House impeaches, the extent of powers of the Senate at that point are to remove the individual from office and disqualify him from ever holding an elected office again. However, the impeached individual is still liable to trial and punishment for the offence he committed under existing laws. Although the Senate did not remove Clinton from office he was still cited for contempt of court, of which he later plea bargained.

Section 4:

The Times, Places and Manner of holding Elections for Senators and Representatives, shall be prescribed in each State by the Legislature thereof; but the Congress may at any time by Law make or alter such Regulations, except as to the Places of chusing Senators.

The time, place and manner of holding elections for Senators and Representatives will be decided by each state legislature. Congress does, however, retain the power to alter the times and manner.

The Congress shall assemble at least once in every Year, and such Meeting shall be (on the first Monday in December,)[14] unless they shall by Law appoint a different Day.

Congress shall meet at least once a year.

Section 5:

Each House shall be the Judge of the Elections, Returns and Qualifications of its own Members...

Both houses shall be the final arbiter as to the qualifications of its elected members. In other words, when the people elect a Senator or Representative it is up to each house to determine if that individual meets the constitutional requirement for office. Take for example in 1934, a twenty nine year old, Rush Holt was elected to the Senate. As we saw in section 3 above, no one could become a Senator until he had attained the age of thirty. Mr. Holt agreed to wait until his 30th birthday to take the oath of

---

[14] Changed by section 2 of the Twentieth Amendment, to noon on the third day of January every year

office. Another more recent example, Barack Hussein Obama was never vetted by the Senate.

...and a Majority of each shall constitute a Quorum to do Business; but a smaller number may adjourn from day to day, and may be authorized to compel the Attendance of absent Members, in such Manner, and under such Penalties as each House may provide.

A majority must be present to do business; in the Senate that number would be 51, in the House it would require 218 members to be present. Smaller numbers can adjourn and compel the attendance of absent members under the rules that have been promulgated by each house.

Each House may determine the Rules of its Proceedings, punish its Members for disorderly behavior, and, with the Concurrence of two thirds, expel a Member.

This clause gives each house the authority to police itself by establishing rules and punishment. In today's Congress that is akin to the fox determining the rules of the chicken pen.

Each House shall keep a Journal of its Proceedings, and from time to time publish the same, excepting such Parts as may in their Judgment require Secrecy; and the Yeas and Nays of the Members of either House on any question shall, at the Desire of one fifth of those Present. Be entered on the Journal.

Congress must meet openly and with transparency. Secrecy only if such proceedings would be harmful for the country such as in time of war. Unless, of course, you are a member of today's congress who love to give aid and comfort to the enemy by broadcasting date and time of withdrawals during times of conflict and war.

Neither House, during the Session of Congress shall, without the Consent of the other, adjourn for more than three days, nor to any other Place than that in which the two Houses shall be sitting.

Neither house may adjourn for more than three days without the consent of the other, also they may not meet anywhere except in the capitol without the consent of the other.

Section 6:

The Senators and Representatives shall receive a Compensation for their Services, to be ascertained by Law, and paid out of the Treasury of the United States.[15]

All Senators and Representatives shall receive a pay check, and you guessed it, they get to determine how much and we have to pay it. The Constitution says nothing about benefits and pensions, because they were not to be there long enough for such nonsense. Speaking of benefits; wonder why they have a market based retirement plan and all we get is social security, run by them. Do they think they are better than us?

They shall in all Cases, except Treason, Felony and Breach of the Peace, be privileged from Arrest during their Attendance at the Session of their respective Houses, and in going to and returning from the same; and for any Speech or Debate in either House, they shall not be questioned in any other Place.

Now, perhaps we can understand why so many congressmen have thousands of dollars in unpaid parking tickets. If they are not accused of Treason, Felony or Breach of the Peace

---

[15] This would be modified by the 27th amendment whereby any change in compensation would not take place until after the next Congressional election.

they are privileged. The latter part protects congressmen from prosecution of slander for anything said in Speech or Debate when done as part of their duties in either House.

No Senator or Representative shall, during the Time for which he was elected, be appointed to any civil Office under the Authority of the United States, which shall have been created, or the Emoluments whereof shall have been increased during such time; and no Person holding any Office under the United States, shall be a Member of either House during his Continuance in Office.

No Senator or Representative can resign to take a position in government that may have been created that has a higher pay. Likewise, any person holding office under the United States cannot be a member of congress. Simply put, one cannot hold two jobs at once. This issue was brought to the forefront in 1937 when Senator Hugo Black was appointed to the Supreme Court. Congress had recently passed a Supreme Court retirement law increasing the emoluments of the office of Supreme Court Justices. Since Hugo Black was a sitting Senator it was initially argued that he was ineligible for the appointment. However, after much debate in Congress, it was determined that because Black was 51 years old he would not receive the increased pension for at least 19 years; many years after his Senate term would expire.

As an aside, allow me to show you how slick our congressmen are. When Hillary Clinton accepted the position of Sectary of State she would be resigning from her lower paying Senate seat to accept a higher paying position in the State department; clearly a violation of the Constitution. However, our squeaky clean congressmen will simply convene and reduce the pay scale for Secretary of State. Therefore, technically, Hillary

Clinton will not be in violation because she will be leaving her higher paying job for a lower paying one. They have such great respect for our Constitution.

Section 7:

All bills for raising Revenue shall originate in the House of Representatives; but the Senate may propose or concur with Amendments as on other Bills.

When our Congressmen want to tax us the bill must originate in the House of Representatives, whereby the Senate may then agree or introduce amendments. Of course, history has shown that no Congressman be he a Senator or Representative is ever in disagreement when it comes to taxing us to pay their graft. The motto of our Congressman is:

1. If it moves, tax it.
2. If it doesn't move, tax it.
3. If it falls in neither category, tax it.[16]

Every Bill which shall have passed the House of Representatives and the Senate, shall, before it become a Law, be presented to the President of the United States: If he approve he shall sign it, but if not he shall return it, with his Objections to that House in which it shall have originated, who shall enter the Objections at large on their Journal, and proceed to reconsider it. If after such Reconsideration two thirds of that House shall agree to pass the Bill, it shall be sent, together with the Objections, to the other House, by which it shall likewise be reconsidered, and if approved by two thirds of that House, it shall become a Law. But in

---

[16] Martin L Gross, The Tax Racket

all such Cases the Votes of both Houses shall be determined by yeas and Nays, and the Names of the Persons voting for and against the Bill shall be entered on the Journal of each House respectively.

Any bill passed by Congress must first be signed by the President before it becomes law. If the President shall disagree he can simply veto the bill, returning it to Congress with his objections. A two-thirds majority of both houses are necessary to override a Presidential veto.

If any Bill shall not be returned by the President within ten Days (Sundays excepted) after it shall have been presented to him, the Same shall be a Law, in like Manner as if he had signed it, unless the Congress by their Adjournment prevent its Return, in which Case it shall not be a Law.

The President has ten days to sign the bill, except Sundays, or it becomes law automatically. However, if the President returns the bill within ten days, except Sundays, and Congress is not in session the bill cannot become law.

Every Order, Resolution, or Vote to which the Concurrence of the Senate and House of Representatives may be necessary (except on a question of Adjournment) shall be presented to the President of the United States; and before the Same shall take Effect, shall be approved by him, or being disapproved by him, shall be repassed by two thirds of the Senate and House of Representatives, according to the Rules and Limitations prescribed in the Case of a Bill.

The founding fathers anticipated the possible abuse by the legislature in passing a "bill" without the consent of the President by calling it an order, or resolution. This section closes that gap by requiring all actions of Congress to be approved by the President.

Any order, resolution or vote other than a bill which might require the concurrence of both the Senate and House, with the exception of adjournment, (again recognizing the separation of powers between the Executive and legislative branch the founding fathers made it very clear the President could not adjourn Congress), must also be approved by the President. If not approved by him these resolutions must also gather a two-thirds majority to override the President's decision, much like the procedure for a bill. In other words, all regulations must also have congressional approval and Presidential concurrence. But, that is not a problem with this group, they love to regulate our lives.

The following section describes the entire parameters of the Federal government. Section 8 lays out the twenty one duties of Congress. Keep in mind if it is not specifically stated in the Constitution as a power of the Federal Government then it is relegated to the individual States. This section is often referred to as the enumerated powers clause. "...it is to be remembered that the general government is not to be charged with the whole power of making and administering laws. Its jurisdiction is limited to certain enumerated objects..."[17] "There is nothing absurd or impracticable in the idea of a league or alliance between independent nations for certain defined purposes precisely stated in a treaty regulating all the details of time, place, circumstance, and quantity; leaving nothing to future discretion."[18] Only an Ivy League lawyer could confuse

---

[17] James Madison, Federalists no. 14
[18] Alexander Hamilton, Federalists no. 15 defining the idea of Government

these two statements. Make no mistake about it; this section and the tenth amendment make it crystal clear if a power is not demonstratively stated to be within the purview of the Federal Government it is clearly reserved for the States. In other words, *'when in doubt the states win out.'*

Section 8:

One: **The Congress shall have Power To lay and collect Taxes, Duties, Imposts and Excises,**
The founders neither envisioned nor contemplated an ever growing welfare state. Monies necessary to finance the twenty-one duties of the federal government were sufficiently raised by taxing imported goods, (duties and impost). An additional tax on internal commodities such as alcohol and tobacco was also levied, (excise).

Two: **to pay the Debts and provide for the common Defense and general Welfare of the United States;**
In order to pay the debts of the United States, taxes were typically placed on imports and exports as we just learned. Furthermore, the purpose of said taxes was to supply and support a standing Army to protect the "General Welfare" of the United States. The two most misunderstood clauses in the Constitution are the "General Welfare" clause and the "Commerce" clause. We will concern ourselves with the Commerce Clause later in this Article. But as for the "General Welfare" here is what Madison had to say: "With respect to the two words 'General Welfare' I have always regarded them as qualified by the detail of powers connected with them. To take them in a literal and unlimited sense would be a metamorphosis of the Constitution into a character which there is a host of proofs

was not contemplated by its creators."[19] Madison is referring to himself, Alexander Hamilton, John Jay and all the delegates from the Constitutional Convention during the summer of 1787. In other words, if you are not a lawyer "General Welfare" is understood as being restricted to only the twenty one powers enumerated in this section. To that end, it was recognized by the framers that a strong military should be first and foremost. The need for a strong military was so paramount that it was the central topic of discussion in the third, fourth, fifth, sixth and seventh federalist papers.

Madison also says, "The powers delegated by the proposed constitution to the federal government are few and defined. Those which are to remain in the State governments are numerous and indefinite. The former will be exercised principally on external objects, as war, peace, negotiation, and foreign commerce... The powers reserved to the several States will extend to all the objects which, in the ordinary course of affairs, concern the lives, liberties, and properties of the people, and the internal order, improvement, and prosperity of the State. The operation of the federal government will be most extensive and important in times of war and danger."[20] Clearly, the General Welfare clause is a limiting clause. In other words EPA, OSHA, DEM, Education, Welfare, HUD, HHS et.al. and literally hundreds of Federal organizations are unconstitutional. Go to USA.gov to see a list of all the Federal Government agencies that are unconstitutional. Remember unconstitutional equals illegal. All of these functions belong to the states. "...the powers of the general government should be limited, and that, beyond this

---

[19] Written in a letter to James Robertson
[20] Federalists 45

limit, the States should be left in possession of their sovereignty and independence."[21]

The founders were adamantly opposed to federal regulation because with it they saw a nation destroying itself from within. In Federalists 21 Hamilton says, "The attempt, therefore, to regulate the contributions of the members of a confederacy by any such rule, cannot fail to be productive of glaring inequality and extreme oppression. This inequality would, of itself be sufficient in America to work the eventual destruction of the Union." In other words the shear ignorance of today's Congressmen is exemplified in that single statement. Our Federal government (that is my congressman and yours) are running rough shod over us and the Constitution. The Federal Government (again mine and your congressman) should be seen but not heard, their job is to protect us in time of war and danger and to conduct foreign policy. Case closed!

Three: **but all Duties, Imposts and Excises shall be uniform throughout the United States;**

All taxes would be uniform throughout the United States. In other words, the excise tax on tobacco in Virginia would be the same in any other state. There would be no taxing one entity more or less than another. Today's Congress Men and Women love to pass out favors with our money by taxing some but not others. Note there is no mention of personal income tax, this would be added with the 16th Amendment.

Four: **To borrow money on the credit of the United States;**

Congress can borrow money and use the Several States and their population as collateral. But, once again, only as it pertains to these twenty one enumerated powers.

---

[21] Federalists 40

Five: **To regulate Commerce with foreign Nations, and among the several States, and with the Indian Tribes;**

The Commerce clause, along with the General Welfare clause as noted above and also the Bill of Rights, we might add, have been the most argued parts of the constitution. These two clauses have been used to expand the Federal Government to something the founding fathers never contemplated. The commerce clause is not difficult to understand. It clearly says, "To regulate Commerce with foreign Nations, and *among* the several States…" Notice it clearly says *among*, **NOT** *within* the several States. There was a very good reason for this distinction. Hamilton, Madison and Jay were well versed in history. As a matter of fact in Federalists six and seven Hamilton goes into great detail about the history of some of the great and past nation states and the single greatest reason for their ultimate demise. As it turns out it was the need for strong armies for the protection of commerce.

History is replete with wars fought over the protection of commerce or annexing the commerce of a rival nation. In Federalist six and seven Hamilton says, "The competitions of commerce would be another fruitful source of contention." The founders sought to eliminate or reduce this interstate rival or (contention) as he puts it, whereby one state might impose import taxes on another. Under the Articles of Confederation[22] individual states not only would erect protectionist trade barriers with foreign countries but also against other states. Therefore, we have the above commerce clause; it has absolutely nothing to do with commerce within a sovereign state, even if that commerce extended into other states, so long as each state was

---

[22] The ruling documents of the 13 states prior to the adoption of the Constitution

not engaged in protectionism or excise taxes. The entrepreneur was free to extend his or her product as far as a free market would accept it, without the onerous rules, regulations and taxes we see today. The sole purpose of the Commerce clause was the elimination of trade barriers among the states. Today the commerce clause is used to impose restrictions on the individual, the entrepreneur and corporations.

Six: **To establish an uniform Rule of Naturalization and uniform Laws on the subject of Bankruptcies throughout the United States;**

Congress will establish rules and laws of Naturalization and Bankruptcies that will be uniformly applied throughout the United States. Obviously, with our open borders policy, today's Congress hasn't read this far in the Constitution.

Seven: **To coin Money, regulate the Value thereof, and of foreign Coin, and fix the Standard of Weights and Measures;**

As with five above, it would be tremendously confusing and counterproductive if individual states had the authority to coin money and chose their own standard of weights and measures. Therefore, for the sake of continuity and simplicity these functions were left to Congress.

Eight: **To provide for the Punishment of counterfeiting the Securities and current Coin of the United States;**

Obviously, the ability to exact punishment gives strength and credence to Congresses' function to coin money.

Nine: **To establish Post Offices and Post Roads;**

Now you and I would clearly understand this to mean our congress men and women would have the authority to build Post Offices along with the Highway and road system in which to transport the mail. However, today's Federal Department of

Transportation has some 60,000 employees with the following agencies:

FAA Federal Aviation Administration
FHWA Federal Highway Administration
FMCSA Federal Motor Carrier Safety Administration
FRA Federal Railroad Administration
FTA Federal Transit Administration
MARAD Maritime Administration
NHTSA National Highway Traffic Safety Administration
OIG Office of Inspector General
PHMSA Pipeline and Hazardous Materials Safety Administration
RITA Research and Innovative Technology Administration
SLSDC Saint Lawrence Seaway Development Corporation
STB Surface Transportation Board

None of which are constitutional, no wonder federal gasoline taxes are 18.4 cents a gallon.

Ten: **To promote the Progress of Science and useful Arts, by securing for limited Times to Authors and Inventors the exclusive Right to their respective Writings and Discoveries;**

Allows authors and inventors to protect their work with copyright laws and patents; this *does not* give my Congressman or yours the authority to spend our money on science, medicine, inventions, art, music or anything. For if they were smart enough to be entrepreneurs, they wouldn't be Congressmen. It simply means government is to get out of the way and let the entrepreneur go.

Eleven: **To constitute Tribunals inferior to the Supreme Court;**

To setup and establish a court system other than the Supreme Court, from which we get our entire federal court system.

Twelve: **To define and punish Piracies and Felonies committed on the high Seas, and Offenses against the Law of Nations;**

At the time of the Constitution Piracies were well understood and as with the commerce clause it was deemed chaotic to allow the several states to pursue and punish piracies on the high seas, therefore this power was delegated to the Congress. It was also understood that for a nation to be in good standing in the family of nations it would be necessary to enforce the laws of nations. As nations around the world began to engage in commerce there was a basic understanding of precepts that nations would agree upon. By way of example, if an individual murdered another on the high seas, that incident would not only fall under the definition of Piracy; it would also be consistent with punishment as to the laws of Nations. The mere fact that someone was on the high seas and on no territorial property of any country did not exempt them from the laws of nations.

Thirteen: **To declare War, grant Letters of Marque and Reprisal, and make Rules concerning Captures on Land and Water;**

First let us define "Letters of Marque": This is simply a written authority by a government to a private person, which today is our military personal, to seize the subjects or goods of a foreign nation. "Reprisal", is defined as an act or practice in international law allowing force, usually short of war, to affect

"Letters of Marque." Once again we see a desire to maintain continuity in a newly formed nation whereby a declaration of war and the ability to seize foreign goods or subjects would be the authority of a single body, the Congress; unless, of course, you are Barack Hussein Obama, who ignored congress and sought the advice and consent of the United Nation before attacking Libya. Although, let us not be so quick to place all the blame on Mr. Obama. He could not have done this without a submissive Congress.

To give this clause force it would also be necessary to allow congress alone to make the rules of war and Letters of Marque. Example: The ACLU (American Civil Liberties Union) has successfully lobbied the Supreme Court to give combatants captured on the field of battle in Afghanistan and Iraq access to our Constitutional privileges'. This directly contravenes the Constitution by usurping the power from Congress as stated in this clause. This is not only wrong, it is idiocy.

Fourteen: **To raise and support Armies, but no Appropriation of Money to that Use shall be for a longer Term than two Years;**

"The authorities essential to the common defense are these: to raise armies; to build and equip fleets; to prescribe rules for the government of both; to direct their operations; to provide for their support. These powers ought to exist without limitations…"

"…it must be admitted, as a necessary consequence, that there can be no limitation of that authority which is to provide for the defense and protection of the community, in any matter essential to its efficacy that is, in any matter essential to the FORMATION, DIRECTION, or SUPPORT of the NATIONAL FORCES." [23]

---

[23] Federalist 23

It follows from the above that military tribunals and places such as Guantanamo Bay are not only necessary but Constitutional. For how can the community be protected by allowing enemies caught on the battle field access to our Constitutional Privileges? Let us not forget the Constitution is to protect the rights of the citizens of America not those who would attack us.

It also follows that if congress has the authority to wage war then it must have the ability and resources to support those armies. Yes gentleman, the draft is Constitutional.[24] However, the two year limitation on appropriations was to keep congress actively involved in the activities of war. Therefore, the merits of a war had to be reviewed and debated every two years.

Fifteen: **To provide and maintain a Navy;**

A navy was deemed indispensible to the defense of our coast and maritime trade. Notice the use of maritime trade in this definition comes from Federalist 11. Once again commerce and a strong military were so inexorably woven that they are central topics for Federalists papers eleven, twelve, thirteen and fourteen. A major concern on the minds of the founding fathers through the first 14 Federalist papers was a strong military for the protection of our "General Welfare" and "Commerce".

Sixteen: **To make Rules for the Government and Regulation of the land and naval Forces;**

The authority to make rules and regulations for governing the land and naval forces would lie directly with congress.

Seventeen: **To provide for calling forth the Militia to execute the Laws of the Union, suppress Insurrections and repel Invasions;**

---

[24] See Appendix: The Draft

It becomes incumbent on us at this point to define "Militia", for we will see it again in the context of the second amendment. Militia comes from the Latin meaning military service; it is simply a body of citizens who are organized for military service. Well then one might ask if the Militia is nothing more than military service weren't they, in fact, established under clause fourteen and fifteen. Not exactly, for the Militia to our founding fathers was much like the National Guard today. The National Guard (Militia) would be used to maintain law and order within the several states. The Militia is under control of the Governors where the Army and Navy are under command of the President. The intention here is clearly not to have a national armed force interfering with the Sovereign States.

Eighteen: **To provide for organizing, arming, and disciplining, the Militia, and for governing such Part of them as may be employed in the Service of the United States, reserving to the States respectively, the Appointment of the Officers, and the Authority of training the Militia according to the discipline prescribed by Congress.**

Although the State Governors would be in charge of the Militia (National Guard) at the state level, the founders also recognized them to be a valuable asset to the defense of the Country in the event of major international crises. In essence the Militia (National Guard) is a reserve army. For that reason it was wisely determined that they should be trained in the like manner of the United States Armed Forces so in the event of a call to service by the Federal Government they would already be trained in a manner consistent with the Regular Army.

By way of example, Governors can call into service the National Guard (Militia) but not the Army. On the other hand the Federal Government can call up the National Guard (Militia) to aid the Regular Army but cannot use the Regular Army to invade a Sovereign State.

Nineteen: **To exercise exclusive Legislation in all Cases whatsoever, over such District (not exceeding ten Miles square) as may, by Cession of particular States, and the Acceptance of Congress, become the Seat of the Government of the United States,**

Establishes a ten square mile district known today as The District of Columbia or in common parlance Washington D.C. This is not a state, but rather, a Federal District that is the seat of the Federal Government which is run by Congress. Washington D.C. has one of the highest crime rates in America, but that is only while Congress is in session; and these people think they can run our health care system. All the talk about making it a State would require an amendment to the Constitution.

Twenty: **and to exercise like Authority over all Places purchased by the Consent of the Legislature of the State in which the Same shall be, for the Erection of Forts, Magazines, Arsenals, dockyards, and other needful Buildings;**

This clause gives the Federal Government Authority over all buildings, forts, magazines, arsenals, dockyards and other needful buildings necessary to maintain an army, navy and carry on federal business. Therefore it is clearly prohibited by the Constitution for the Federal Government to claim lands such as National Parks and anything not directly related to the defense and operation of the Federal Government. You got it! The Federal government cannot constitutionally prevent States such as Alaska from drilling for oil because some area is deemed a national park. Obviously, today's governors only care about maintaining power and good graces with the President and Congress than fighting for the Constitution.

Consider Alexander Hamilton's admonition toward an overbearing federal government in Federalists 33 when he says, "If the federal government should overpass the just bounds of its authority and make a tyrannical use of its powers, the people…must appeal to the standard they have formed, and take such measures to redress the injury done to the Constitution as the exigency may suggest and prudence justify." The State Governors would be well within their Constitutional powers to ignore Congress and drill if they so choose.

Twenty-one: **To make all Laws which shall be necessary and proper for carrying into Execution the foregoing Powers, and all other Powers vested by this Constitution in the Government of the United States, or in any Department or Officer thereof.**

This clause gives Congress authority to enforce the enumerated powers through legislation. Once again, that would include a military draft.

Section 9:

The Migration or Importation of such Persons as any of the States now existing shall think proper to admit, shall not be prohibited by the Congress prior to the Year one thousand eight hundred and eight, but a Tax or duty may be imposed on such Importation, not exceeding ten dollars for each Person.

To understand the inclusion of this paragraph in the Constitution it is necessary to recall what the political atmosphere was during the debates leading to its ratification. The North was steadfastly opposed to slavery while the South, particularly South Carolina and Georgia, were in favor. The North wanted strong control over slavery in order to eventually eliminate it while the South wanted no governmental control. Therefore, the above compromise was agreed upon.[25] During the ratification process this clause was necessary to gain the acceptance of the South. After a period of twenty years this same Constitution allowed for the eventual elimination of slavery. The United States would be the first Western Nation to abolish slavery.

The Privilege of the Writ of Habeas Corpus shall not be suspended, unless when in Cases of Rebellion or Invasion the public Safety may require it.

Too often in the past ruling parties would imprison their political opponents without charge. The Privilege of the Writ of Habeas Corpus Prevents citizens from being held under arrest for an indefinite period; in most cases charges must be made within twenty four to forty eight hours or the individual must be released. The only exceptions were in the event of rebellion or invasion when public safety was jeopardized. This provision was utilized by President Lincoln during the Civil War.

No Bill of Attainder or ex post facto Law shall be passed.

A bill of attainder is to administer punishment to an individual without trial; this clause prevents any citizen from being so punished. An ex post facto law is simply a law passed today cannot be retroactively applied. In other words, if for example, you fail to tip your waitress today but tomorrow a law is passed that says you must under penalty of law tip your waitress, you will not be subject to that law for your actions yesterday.

---

[25] The thirteenth amendment rendered this clause moot.

No Capitation, or other direct, Tax shall be laid, unless in Proportion to the Census or Enumeration herein before directed to be taken.[26]

Historically, a direct tax or capitation tax was understood to be a direct tax on the individual, or a head tax. The founding fathers would have none of this. The so called head tax would be unconstitutional. However, the sixteenth Amendment would change all of that allowing a head tax in proportion to ones income.

No Tax or Duty shall be laid on Articles exported from any State. No Preference shall be given by any Regulation of Commerce or Revenue to the Ports of one State over those of another; nor shall Vessels bound to, or from, one State, be obliged to enter, clear, or pay Duties in another.

We must remember James Madison's admonition that, "The powers delegated by the proposed Constitution to the federal government are few and defined. Those which are to remain in the state governments are numerous and indefinite."[27] These two clauses are consistent with the commerce clause and Madison's admonition above where they simply define in detail what the States cannot do with regards to commerce. No taxes shall be levied on state exports; water vessels can move from state to state without duties or preferential treatment by the several states. The trucking industry today pay a myriad of taxes as they move from state to state.

No Money shall be drawn from the Treasury, but in Consequence of Appropriations made by Law; and regular

---

[26] Changed by the sixteenth Amendment.
[27] Federalist 45

Statement and Account of the Receipts and Expenditures of all public Money shall be published from time to time.

Requires transparency by the Federal Government; no monies are to be withdrawn from the general treasury that are not determined by law and requires a statement of account to be published. Sounds simple enough, however, try to get your arms around the thousands of pages of the Social Security Administration, Medicare, Medicaid, Welfare, and earmarks, none of which are constitutional. So much for Madison's admonition "The powers delegated by the proposed Constitution to the federal government are few and defined."

No Title of Nobility shall be granted by the United States; And no Person holding any Office of Profit or Trust under them, shall, without the Consent of the Congress, accept of any present, Emolument, Office, or Title, of any kind whatever, from any King, Prince or foreign State.

On July 4, 1776 the thirteen colonies issued the Declaration of Independence stating in part they found it necessary to, "... alter their former Systems of Government. The history of the present King of Great Britain is a history of repeated injuries and usurpations, all having in direct object the establishment of an absolute Tyranny over these States." The above clause clearly creates the separation of a government run by nobility of any kind. The founders did, however, allow for consent of Congress for honorary titles only.

Section 10:

No State shall enter into any Treaty, alliance, or Confederation; grant Letters of Marque and Reprisal; coin Money; emit Bills of Credit; make any Thing but gold and silver Coin a Tender in Payment of Debts; pass any

Bill of Attainder, ex post facto Law, or Law impairing the Obligation of Contracts, or grant any Title of Nobility.

We learned in section 8 enumerated power number 13 only the United States Government shall have the power to enter treaties, alliances or confederations and grant letters of Marque and Reprisal. This will be codified by the tenth amendment whereby the United States Government will have only the powers that are delegated to it. Furthermore, only gold and silver would be used in payment of debt. Also, as seen in section 9 above, with the United States Government, the individual states cannot pass a Bill of Attainder, ex post facto Law, impair contracts or grant any title of Nobility. During the Revolutionary period lenders were not allowed to collect debts over a stated period of time. Known as the contracts clause, it is this clause that allows us to buy homes, automobiles and other high end items on time; it also prevents States from altering a contract once in place.

No State shall, without the Consent of the Congress, lay any Imposts or Duties on Imports or Exports, except what may be absolutely necessary for executing it's inspection Laws: and the net Produce of all Duties and Imposts, laid by any State on Imports or Exports, shall be for the Use of the Treasury of the United States; and all such Laws shall be subject to the Revision and Controul of the Congress.

No state will impose duties on imports or exports except for an amount necessary to finance inspection laws, but all duties will be subject to the control of Congress.

No State shall, without the Consent of Congress lay any duty of Tonnage, keep Troops, or Ships of War in time of Peace, enter into any Agreement or Compact with another

State, or with a foreign Power, or engage in War, unless actually invaded, or in such imminent Danger as will not admit of delay.

Duties on tonnage into and out of the several states are the responsibility of congress. Troops, Ships of War and compacts are the responsibility of Congress. No state may engage in war, the only exception would be for example, if Mexico attacked Texas, the Texans would be able to defend themselves without waiting for approval from Congress. The founding fathers would be appalled at a federal government suing a sovereign state for protecting its citizens; as the Obama administration has done with Arizona.

CHAPTER 3

ARTICLE II:

Section 1:

The executive Power shall be vested in a President of the United States of America. He shall hold his Office during the Term of four Years, and, together with the Vice-President chosen for the same Term, be elected, as follows:
This clause establishes the executive branch of government consisting of a President and Vice-President whose terms shall be for four years.

Each State shall appoint, in such Manner as the legislature thereof may direct, a Number of Electors, equal to the whole Number of Senators and Representatives to which the State may be entitled in the Congress: but no Senator or Representative, or Person holding an Office of Trust or Profit under the United States, shall be appointed an Elector.
This clause establishes the Electoral College. Each state shall have the same number of electors as the sum of Senators

and Representatives. For example, Ohio has two Senators and sixteen Representatives; therefore they have eighteen Electoral College votes. Furthermore, those who are electors can hold no other position. Currently there are 538 Electors which include three from the District of Columbia.

The following ten clauses of section one are listed in bold italics without separation, with a single definition after the passage simply to maintain historical accuracy, for the entire passage is changed by the twelfth Amendment.

The Electors shall meet in their respective States, and vote by Ballot for two Persons, of whom one at least shall not be an Inhabitant of the same State with themselves.

And they shall make a List of all the Persons voted for, and of the Number of Votes for each; which List they shall sign and certify, and transmit sealed to the Seat of the Government of the United States, directed to the President of the Senate.

The President of the Senate shall, in the Presence of the Senate and House of Representatives, open all the Certificates, and the Votes shall then be counted. The Person having the greatest Number of Votes shall be the President, if such Number be a Majority of the whole Number of Electors appointed; and if there be more than one who have such Majority, and have an equal Number of Votes, then the House of Representatives shall immediately chuse by Ballot one of them for President; and if no Person have a Majority, then from the five highest on the List the said House shall in like manner chuse the President.

But in chusing the President, the Votes shall be taken by States, the Representation from each State having one Vote; a quorum for this Purpose shall consist of a Member or Members from two-thirds of the States, and a Majority of all the States shall be necessary to a Choice.

In every Case, after the Choice of the President, the Person having the greatest Number of Votes of the Electors shall be the Vice President.

But if there should remain two or more who have equal Votes, the Senate shall chuse from them by Ballot the Vice President.[28]

When the Electors, in each state, meet they will vote for two persons; both of those persons cannot be from the same state as themselves. The list of persons voted for shall be sealed, certified and sent to the President of the Senate. The President of the Senate shall open all the certificates in the presences of the Senate and House of Representatives and count the votes. The person with the greatest number of votes shall be the President, provided he has a majority. If more than one person shall have a majority and they are tied, the House of Representative shall choose. If no one has a majority then the House of Representatives shall choose from the five highest vote getters. If the election is forced to the House of Representatives the Electoral College is out of the picture and each state shall have as many votes as they have representatives. For a quorum to occur two-thirds of the states shall be present with at least one member. The President shall be chosen by a majority of those states present. After choosing the President the next person on the list with the highest number of votes shall be Vice-President. If there is a tie in votes the Senate shall chose from this list the Vice President.

---

[28] Changed by the Twelfth Amendment.

The Congress may determine the Time of chusing the Electors, and the Day on which they shall give their Votes; which Day shall be the same throughout the United States. For the sake of consistency it would be the duty of Congress to determine the time for choosing the electors. Congress would also chose the day the electors would cast their votes.

No person except a natural born Citizen, or a Citizen of the United States, at the time of the Adoption of this Constitution, shall be eligible to the Office of President; neither shall any Person be eligible to that Office who shall not have attained to the Age of thirty-five years, and been fourteen years a Resident within the United States. The qualifications for President were only three; (1) attain the age of 35, (2) be a resident of the United States for 14 years and (3) be a natural born citizen. The framers specifically understood the ramifications of foreign birth. The United States and its Constitution was a bold new experiment. It was born out of a unique American perspective and understanding. There was nothing else on earth quite like it. For it to remain uniquely American it was necessary for its leaders to be immersed in the education and traditions of those values. Remember, the single greatest impetus for this new land was to separate itself from the rest of the world. It is not our heritage to follow, but to lead. Moving to emulate others is easy and cowardly. A desire to lead and remain "That shining city on a hill," as portrayed by President Reagan is all but lost when our leaders are embarrassed by our success and would rather return to a past and pursue mediocrity and appeasement. In Federalists 62 Madison speaks directly to the natural born issue when he said they, "…should have reached a period of life most likely to supply these advantages; and which, participating immediately in transactions with foreign nations, ought to be exercised by none who are not thoroughly weaned from the prepossessions and habits incident to foreign birth and education." Clearly, a presidential candidate who during the campaign referred to his Muslim religion[29] on one occasion and the 57 states of America[30] on another as did Barack Hussein Obama is not one who has been, 'thoroughly weaned from the prepossessions and habits incident to foreign birth and education.' The founding fathers clearly understood natural born to be from parents who were citizens of the United States and born on United States soil or US possessions. Only lawyers or judges with Ivy League educations will fail to understand this obvious connection. Once again we are reminded of Thomas Sowell's admonition, "Academic pedigree is no grantor of useful knowledge."

The simple truth behind the reasoning for minimal requirements to the Presidency, the Vice-Presidency, the Senate and the House of Representatives was the founding fathers never envisioned a Federal Government with career politicians. The purpose of seeking office was to serve the country. It was thought that people from all walks of life would come to Washington, serve and return to their communities. After all, the Constitution was only twenty-seven pages and the duties of the Federal Government were limited, therefore service in the Federal Government was only limited to the twenty-one duties enumerated in Article I, section 8. George Washington refused to accept a wage for his service.

The reason for being a natural born citizen was to prevent foreigners from gaining access to our Constitution for other

---

[29] September 7, 2008 on ABC's This Week with George Stephanopoules.
[30] May 9, 2008 at Campaign event in Beaverton Orgon.

ambitious or corrupt interests. Also, a more important reason perhaps is our country, its Declaration of Independence and its Constitution are deeply rooted in the Judo-Christian values and traditions. The founding fathers understood the danger of having foreign interlopers with values and traditions contradictory to our own founding. The interest of those in the Federal Government should be aligned with the Constitution whose duties would be limited and easily executed. The heavy lifting would be the responsibility of the States.

In Case of the Removal of the President from Office, or of his Death, Resignation, or Inability to discharge the Powers and Duties of the said Office, the Same shall devolve on the Vice President, and the Congress may by Law provide for the Case of Removal, Death, Resignation or Inability, both of the President and Vice President, declaring what officer shall then act as President, and such Officer shall act accordingly, until the Disability be removed, or a President shall be elected.[31]

If the President, for any reason, is unable to perform his duties the Vice-President shall assume those duties. In the event of both the President and Vice-President being unable to perform the executive duties then as per Article I, section 3, the President pro tempore of the Senate will act in the executive capacity. If there is no President pro tempore in the Senate, the duties fall to the Speaker of the House of Representatives, until a President can be elected.

The President shall, at stated Times, receive for his Services, a Compensation, which shall neither be increased nor diminished during the Period for which he shall have

---

[31] Changed by the Twenty-Fifth Amendment.

been elected, and he shall not receive within that Period any other Emolument from the United States, or any of them.

Establishes a salary for the Presidency.

Before he enter on the Execution of his Office, he shall take the following Oath or Affirmation: "I do solemnly swear (or affirm) that I will faithfully execute the Office of President of the United States, and will to the best of my Ability, preserve, protect and defend the Constitution of the United States."

Every President since the New Deal has failed this oath of office.

Section 2:

The President shall be Commander in Chief of the Army and Navy of the United States, and of the Militia of the several States, when called into the actual Service of the United States; he may require the Opinion, in writing, of the principal Officer in each of the executive Departments, upon any subject relating to the Duties of their respective Offices, and he shall have Power to grant Reprieves and Pardons for Offenses against the United States, except in Cases of Impeachment.

The founders recognized the prudence in having the Commander in Chief of the Army, Navy and Militia to be a civilian. The next part of this clause gives authority to the President requiring all executive department heads to issue in writing any opinions generated by their positions. In other words all department heads are responsible to the President. The final part of this clause allows the President to issue Pardons in all offenses except Impeachment.

He shall have Power, by and with the Advice and Consent of the Senate, to make Treaties, provided two thirds of the Senators present concur; and he shall nominate, and by and with the Advice and Consent of the Senate, shall appoint Ambassadors, other public Ministers and Consuls, Judges of the supreme Court, and all other Officers of the United States, whose Appointments are not herein otherwise provided for, and which shall be established by Law: but the Congress may by Law vest the Appointment of such inferior Officers, as they think proper, in the President alone, in the Courts of Law, or in the Heads of Departments.

Another clause lawyers love to obfuscate and cast doubt on. The first part of this clause simply means the President is the sole negotiator of treaties of war, peace and commerce with foreign nations. However, the treaties must then be approved by two-thirds of the Senate. Obviously, he can only negotiate those things that are authorized by the constitution. In other words the President cannot enter into a treaty to circumvent the U.S. Constitution, with or without consent of the Congress. Obama's reliance on the UN to intervene in Libya was unconstitutional.

The next section of this clause gives the president the authority to nominate Supreme Court Judges and inferior court judges needing only a majority of the Senate to confirm. In other words only 51 Senators are needed to approve Supreme Court Judges. A filibuster used to block an appointment would be unconstitutional simply because to end a filibuster requires a two-thirds vote. As we saw above only a majority vote is needed.

The final section of this clause gives the President plenary power to fill lesser officers or department heads. Some have cautioned this to be a dangerous practice because it could lead to tremendous partisan alignments. But let us not forget, the next President can undo all of these appointments by making his own.

The President shall have Power to fill up all Vacancies that may happen during the Recess of the Senate, by granting Commissions which shall expire at the End of their next Session.

If a presidential appointment should become vacant during the recess of the Senate, the President can fill that vacancy without consent until the end of the next Senate session.

Section 3:

He shall from time to time give to the Congress Information of the State of the Union, and recommend to their Consideration such Measures as he shall judge necessary and expedient; he may, on extraordinary Occasions, convene both Houses, or either of them, and in Case of Disagreement between them, with Respect to the Time of Adjournment, he may adjourn them to such Time as he shall think proper; he shall receive Ambassadors and other public Ministers; he shall take Care that the Laws be faithfully executed, and shall Commission all the Officers of the United States.

The first part of this clause we hear every year in the state of the union address. The middle part gives the President authority to convene either or both houses of Congress in an emergency or extraordinary occasion. He can likewise adjourn them at such times he deems proper. For example, when Congress recessed in late 2008 without a vote on drilling for oil, many people urged the President to reconvene them for said vote. This clause gives him that authority, but he chose not to use it.

The next sentence requires no elaboration, for the President is responsible for receiving Ambassadors and heads of State. After all foreign policy is the purview of the President, so it stands to reason he should be the one to receive said dignitaries. The last sentence confines the President to carry out his duties within the constraints of the law. Finally, if he is authorized to appoint Officers of the United States, he shall likewise be responsible for their commission.

Section 4:

The President, Vice President and all civil Officers of the United States, shall be removed from Office on Impeachment for, and Conviction of, Treason, Bribery, or other high Crimes and Misdemeanors.

One would think this article is self-explanatory; however, judging from the Clinton Impeachment apparently it is widely misunderstood. The President, Vice President and all civil officers can be removed from office by impeachment when convicted of four things: one, treason two, bribery, three, high crimes and four, misdemeanors. If you are not a lawyer, this is a perfectly clear statement. However, often during the Clinton impeachment hearings one would hear many in the media say his lying under oath did not rise to the level of high crimes and misdemeanors. The trick here is to link misdemeanors to high crimes. Once the media and Clinton supporters accomplished that link people began to think of a misdemeanor as a high crime. A high crime is a felony, such as grand larceny, assault, murder etc. Certainly, Clinton was not guilty of any such thing. On the other hand when one separates misdemeanors from high crimes as a reason for impeachment the case against Clinton becomes crystal clear. Our forefathers expected the Office of President to be an exemplary citizen therefore he could also be impeached for misdemeanors. Any crime that carries more than a $250 fine or a one year or less prison sentence is considered a misdemeanor. Clinton was found guilty of perjury which carries both a fine and imprisonment as punishment.

CHAPTER 4

ARTICLE III

Section 1

The judicial Power[32] of the United States shall be vested in one supreme Court, and in such inferior Courts as the Congress may from time to time ordain and establish. The Judges, both of the supreme and inferior Courts, shall hold their Offices during good Behaviour, and shall, at stated Times, receive for their Services a Compensation which shall not be diminished during their Continuance in Office.

Although this clause establishes the Federal Court System and their right to compensation, it leaves the bulk of judicial powers to the state governments.

Section 2:

The judicial Power shall extend to all Cases, in Law and Equity, arising under this Constitution, the Laws of the United States, and Treaties made, or which shall be made,

---

[32] See Appendices re: The Judiciary

under their Authority; to all Cases affecting Ambassadors, other public Ministers and Consuls; to all Cases of admiralty and maritime Jurisdiction; to Controversies to which the United States shall be a Party; to Controversies between two or more States; (between a State and Citizens of another State;)[33] between Citizens of different States; between Citizens of the same State claiming Lands under Grants of different States, (and between a State, or the Citizens thereof, and foreign States, Citizens or Subjects.)[34]

The first Congress to meet after ratification of the Constitution in 1789 established the federal court system we have today, under authority of section 1 above. The power of the judiciary would extend to all cases in Law and Equity as pertained to the laws promulgated under the Constitution. Until changed by the eleventh Amendment they also had authority to sit in judgment of cases between a state and citizens of another state; and between a state and the citizens of that state. The reason for the eleventh Amendment was the states viewed this intrusion from the federal government as a gross infringement on state sovereignty.

In all Cases affecting Ambassadors, other public Ministers and Consuls, and those in which a State shall be Party, the supreme Court shall have original Jurisdiction. In all the other Cases before mentioned, the supreme Court shall have appellate Jurisdiction, both as to Law and Fact, with such Exceptions, and under such Regulations as the Congress shall make.

---

[33] Changed by the eleventh Amendment
[34] Ibid

The Supreme Court shall have original Jurisdiction, in all cases affecting Ambassadors, other public Ministers and Consuls, and those in which a State shall be party to. In all other cases the Supreme Court shall have appellate jurisdiction, exceptions can be made as the Congress may by law direct. (Original jurisdiction is the authority of a court to try a case in the first instance and give judgment according to the facts and evidence as opposed to appellate jurisdiction where the case has already been tried but an appeal is made for review.)

An example of original jurisdiction would be if a law promulgated by Congress such as universal health care were to be challenged for constitutionality, it could not be filed in the Supreme Court first. It would, instead, need to be filed in a state court and work its, way through the appeal process whose final stop would be the Supreme Court.

The Trial of all Crimes, except in Cases of Impeachment, shall be by Jury; and such Trial shall be held in the State where the said Crimes shall have been committed; but when not committed within any State, the Trial shall be at such Place or Places as the Congress may by Law have directed.

Gives to all citizens the right of trial by jury except in cases of impeachment; the trial shall also take place in the state where the crime was committed. At the time when the Constitution was adopted there were states and territories, therefore, the last sentence says the trial shall take place where Congress so directs when not committed within any state.

Section 3:

Treason against the United States shall consist only in levying War against them, or in adhering to their Enemies,

giving them Aid and Comfort. No Person shall be convicted of Treason unless on the Testimony of two Witnesses to the same overt Act, or on Confession in open Court.

First, treason against the United States is defined as anyone who commits acts of war against the United States or giving aid and comfort to an enemy. For example these persons can be domestic as in William "Bill" Ayres or foreign such as Osama bin Laden. Second, anyone who gives aid and comfort to our enemies will also be guilty of treason. For example when in September 2007 Senator Charles Schumer from New York said, "...the violence in Anbar has gone down despite the surge, not because of the surge. The inability of American Soldiers to protect these tribes from al Qaeda..." would certainly qualify as giving aid and comfort to our enemies as defined by our forefathers.

The last sentence says to be convicted of treason there must be at least two persons who witnessed the act or the person confesses.

The Congress shall have power to declare the Punishment of Treason, but no Attainder of Treason shall work Corruption of Blood, or Forfeiture except during the Life of the Person attainted

As stated in the foreword to this book the Constitution was written in the common language of the day. Attainder of Treason and corruption of blood were terms commonly used in Old English. An attainder of Treason is a death sentence for one convicted of Treason. Corruption of Blood is an Old English term meaning the blood of the person attained (given the death sentence) was so corrupted by his crimes that he could no longer hold land, nor leave it to heirs, nor could his descendents inherit from him. In other words anyone related to one convicted of treason would also pay a heavy penalty through corruption of blood, meaning they too would somehow be penalized for transgressions of relatives. A corruption of blood could last for decades, affecting the children, grand children, even great grand children. However, this clause prevents the decedents of a corrupted individual from persecution. In other words the descendants of Benedict Arnold would not be held liable for his acts.

CHAPTER 5

ARTICLE IV

Section 1:

Full Faith and Credit shall be given in each State to the public Acts, Records, and judicial Proceedings of every other State. And the Congress may by general Laws prescribe the Manner in which such Acts, Records and Proceedings shall be proved, and the Effect thereof.

Known as the full faith and credit clause, the intended purpose was to enforce judgments among the several states. In other words if a court in Connecticut found someone guilty and was assessed a fine, that individual could not run to Massachusetts to get away from paying. Likewise, if a person was found innocent of a crime in Virginia he could not be charged for that crime in another state. For example, if you live in a state that does not require automobile inspections, you will not be fined for not having one if you visit or drive through a state that does.

Even marriage in one state would be recognized in all the states. However, homosexual unions, may not. Much like the automobile inspection example above; if one lives in a state that does not require an inspection you will not be punished or required to get the inspection in a state that does if you are visiting or passing through. On the other hand, if you chose to move there, then you are choosing to live by their rules.

Homosexual unions are no different. Just because you live in a state that recognizes them does not permit you to force all other states to recognize your particular situation. While this is not a book on social issues the parallels for the marriage issue and the Constitution are stark and require further investigation.

Words mean things. Acquiring a vocabulary allows members of a society to communicate. For example, go to any restaurant in America and ask for a bowl of chili, there is a reasonable expectation you will not receive tomato soup. Ask for a ham sandwich, there is a reasonable expectation it will not be Turkey. Because words mean things, when someone indicates they are married, there is a reasonable expectation they are referring to the opposite sex. It brings to mind the old saying, 'you may call a skunk a rose but it is still going to stink.'

Mine and your congressman will go to great lengths to "obfuscate" the meaning of the Constitution, much like the homosexual lobby is going to great lengths to "obfuscate" the meaning of marriage. The Constitution has a specific meaning, as does the word marriage. When society begins to change the meaning of words to satisfy numerous splinter constituencies, only chaos will follow; therefore the true meaning of such things as marriage and the Constitution become lost in the specious arguments.

Another more egregious example, when Barack Hussein Obama finally produced a birth certificate it proved he was not a natural born citizen. However, the meaning of natural born has been lost therefore his lack of natural born status did not create so much as a yawn. To be natural born is to be born from parents who are both US citizens. A native born individual is born in the US but one or both parents are not a citizen. For example Senator Marco Rubio was born in Florida in 1971; his parents did not become US citizens until 1975. Therefore, he too, is not constitutionally qualified to be President or Vice President. If Brack Hussein Obama's birth certificate is correct, only one of his parents was a US citizen, therefore, by his own admission, he does not constitutionally qualify to be President. If we do not have the will to correct the situation, the Constitution has already been rendered moot.

Section 2:

The Citizens of each State shall be entitled to all Privileges and Immunities of Citizens in the several States.

This clause simply states citizens of the United States can move freely from state to state with no worry of differential treatment. All State and Federal constitutional guarantees and immunities shall apply regardless of what state you moved from or into.

There are, however, two notable exceptions: one, the Privileges and Immunities does not apply to corporations or businesses. Two, the Privileges and Immunities does not apply to state licenses for professional certification, state licenses for hunting and fishing or differential college tuition rates. Such discrepancies are said to be justifiable because they advance legitimate state interest.

A Person charged in any State with Treason, Felony, or other Crime, who shall flee from Justice, and be found in another State, shall on demand of the executive Authority of the State from which he fled, be delivered up, to be removed to the State having Jurisdiction of the Crime.

All states must agree to the extradition of an individual who has fled one state into another for the purpose of avoiding punishment. The governor of the state having jurisdiction of the crime need only inform his counterpart in the opposing state.

(No Person held to Service or Labour in one State, under the Laws thereof, escaping into another, shall, in Consequence of any Law or Regulation therein, be discharged from such Service or Labour, but shall be delivered up on Claim of the Party to whom such Service or Labour may be due.)[35]

Simply put this clause prevented slaves from escaping their bondage into another state. The slave owner had a right to reclaim any such individual. This would all be changed by the thirteenth amendment.

Section 3:

New States may be admitted by the Congress into this Union; but no new State shall be formed or erected within the Jurisdiction of any other State; nor any State be formed by the Junction of two or more States, or parts of States, without the "Consent of the Legislatures of the States concerned as well as of the Congress.

---

[35] Changed by the thirteenth amendment.

This clause establishes the parameters for admitting new States to the Union. If you are not a lawyer this clause is self-explanatory. Any territory that wished to become a state would need congressional approval. Any state formed by the junction of two or more states or the splitting of a state would not only require congressional approval but also the approval of the state. It is interesting to note that West Virginia was formed by splitting from Virginia. When the Civil War broke out in 1861 Virginia seceded from the union. While few of the counties in Western Virginia owned slaves they chose not to secede and remained part of the Union. On June 20, 1863 they were admitted to the Union as West Virginia.

The Congress shall have Power to dispose of and make all needful Rules and Regulations respecting the Territory or other Property belonging to the United States; and nothing in this Constitution shall be so construed as to Prejudice any Claims of the United States, or of any particular State.

Gives Congress the authority to legislate all properties and territories belonging to the United States; for example, States cannot tax Federal property. In Nevada, the Federal Government (Congress) owns or controls some 86.1% of the land; that represents a lot of lost tax revenue for the state. Furthermore, you might be interested to know that in Alaska, Utah and Idaho more than 60% of the land is also owned by the Federal Government (Congress).[36]

Why you might ask does your Congressman and mine need so much land? Your guess is as good as mine. After all we saw in Article 1 section 8 they were only authorized to utilize enough land for "...the Erection of Forts, Magazines, Arsenals, Dockyards, and other needful buildings." Perhaps they purchased

---

[36] Nevada Natural Resources status report web site, 2009.

this land for a naval base; this is clearly an unconstitutional federal land grab. The original intent of this clause was the administration of territories that were not states.

Section 4:

The United States shall guarantee to every State in this Union a Republican Form of Government, and shall protect each of them against Invasion; and on Application of the Legislature, or of the Executive (when the Legislature cannot be convened) against domestic Violence.

A Republican Form of Government is not a democracy it is a representative government where the individual states elect their respective representatives who then go to Congress and vote their conscience. "In a democracy, the people meet and exercise the government in person; in a republic, they assemble and administer it by their representatives and agents."[37] It was an ingenious system whereby mob rule would be relegated to obscurity.

Our founding fathers would be aghast at the obvious mob rule of a 21st century government where the 535 members of congress are ram-roding a plethora of rules, laws and regulations that contravenes everything the people want. Our Congress is frighteningly out of control.

The second part of the first sentence reaffirms Article I, section 8, the first clause where the duty of the Federal Government is to protect each state from invasion by providing, "... for the common Defence."

The final part of this clause prevents the US Military from marching into a sovereign state to put down riots, rebellion or violence without the request of their legislature or executive if the legislature is not in session.

---

[37] James Madison, Federalists 14

CHAPTER 6

ARTICLE V:

The Congress, whenever two thirds of both Houses shall deem it necessary, shall propose Amendments to this Constitution, or, on the Application of the Legislatures of two thirds of the several States, shall call a Convention for proposing Amendments, which, in either Case, shall be valid to all Intents and Purposes, as Part of this Constitution, when ratified by the Legislatures of three fourths of the several States, or by Conventions in three fourths thereof, as the one or the other Mode of Ratification may be proposed by the Congress; Provided that no Amendment which may be made prior to the Year One thousand eight hundred and eight shall in any Manner affect the first and fourth Clauses in the Ninth Section of the first Article; and that no State, without its Consent, shall be deprived of its equal Suffrage in the Senate.

Article five establishes the means of amending the constitution. The process was specifically designed to be difficult to prevent specious changes in the heat of battle. The

Constitution can be amended in two ways. First, there must be two thirds of both Houses of Congress to introduce such amendments, which must then be ratified by three fourths of the Several States.

The second avenue for change is for two thirds of the State legislatures to convene a Constitutional convention and introduce an amendment which must then be ratified by three fourths of the Several States. The last sentence prohibits an amendment before 1808 that would interfere with the first clause of the ninth section of Article I (Slavery) and the fourth clause of the same section and Article (Taxes). Both of these would later be changed through the amendment process.

Two observations to make here; one, some lawyers will make the case that because the Article does not make clear how the amendment proposing convention is to be composed and operated, Congress presumably could determine how the delegates are chosen and provide for other details. This kind of thinking is dangerously wrong. Let us quote Madison once again, "The powers delegated by the proposed Constitution to the Federal government are few and defined. Those which are to remain in the state governments are numerous and indefinite."[38] In other words, *when in doubt, the states win out.*

Our second observation is there are no time constraints placed on ratifying an amendment. It took over two hundred years to ratify the Twenty-Seventh Amendment. However, beginning in the 20th century Congress has corrected this oversight by imposing deadlines for ratification within the body of an amendment.

---

[38] Federalist 45

Barack Hussein Obama has said he found the Constitution fatally flawed.[39] A statement like that from someone who wants to be the leader of the free world is scary. What kind of message does that send our would-be enemies? Well that aside, this lack of time constraint is the only concession this author will make as to flaws in the Constitution.

---

[39] October 27, 2008 youtube interview.

CHAPTER 7

ARTICLE VI:

All Debt contracted and Engagements entered into, before the Adoption of this Constitution, shall be as valid against the United States under this Constitution, as under the Confederation.

Prior to the ratification of the Constitution the Several States were organized by the Articles of Confederation. This first clause, under Article VI was to reaffirm all debts, contracts and engagements that were made under the Articles of Confederation would continue to be recognized under the Constitution.

This Constitution, and the Laws of the United States which shall be made in Pursuance thereof; and all Treaties made, or which shall be made, under the Authority of the United States, shall be the supreme Law of the Land; and the Judges in every State shall be bound thereby, any Thing in the Constitution or Laws of any State to the Contrary notwithstanding.

This clause makes it clear that the Constitution and all laws made pursuant to the Constitution will be the Supreme law of the land. If a state law conflicts with the Constitution the Constitution trumps state law. In other words, when our elected representatives ignor the Constitution, they not only break the law, but they break the Supreme Law of the Land.

The Senators and Representatives before mentioned, and the Members of the several State Legislatures, and all executive and judicial Officers, both of the United States and of the several States, shall be bound by Oath or Affirmation, to support this Constitution; but no religious Test shall ever be required as a Qualification to any Office or public Trust under the United States.

All elected officials of both the Federal Government and State government shall take an oath or affirmation to support and uphold the Constitution. If Barack Hussein Obama thinks it is fatally flawed how can he take an oath to uphold same? Ones religious beliefs shall never be a disqualification to hold office.

CHAPTER 8

ARTICLE VII:

The Ratification of the Conventions of nine States shall be sufficient for the Establishment of this Constitution between the States so ratifying the Same.

Done in Convention by the Unanimous Consent of the States present the Seventeenth Day of September in the Year of our Lord one thousand seven hundred and Eighty seven and of the Independence of the United States of American the Twelfth In Witness whereof We have hereunto subscribed our Names.

The ratification by nine states was sufficient to establish the Constitution as the supreme law of the land. It is interesting to note that of the thirteen states in existence at the time of the constitutional convention Rhode Island was the only state that did not send a delegation to the convention. Although, the twelve states present at the Constitutional Convention ratified the Constitution Rhode Island did eventually ratify it on May 29, 1790.

CHAPTER 9

THE BILL OF RIGHTS

Ratified December 15, 1791 (811days)

Amendments I – X

During the Constitutional Convention debates from May 25 to September 17, 1787 many delegates expressed their concerns regarding the need for a Bill of Rights. Keep in mind these delegates still had a fresh memory of the Revolution fought against the British over civil rights. Although, defenders of the Constitution said a Bill of Rights would not be necessary because all such rights were implicit within the Constitution. Not satisfied with this argument the opposing delegates demanded a Bill of Rights that would specifically identify some of the unalienable rights of its citizens. To that end, the Bill of Rights can be thought of as a grocery list of items that were identified within the Constitution. The Government could neither give these rights nor take them from the people because of the unalienable characteristic of those items.

On September 17, 1787 the delegates adopted the Constitution and sent it to the states for ratification without a Bill of Rights but with the general understanding that a so called Bill of Rights would follow at some later date. In only thirty four days five states ratified the Constitution. However, during the Massachusetts ratification process it looked as though the Constitution would go down in defeat unless and until a Bill of Rights became part of the document. This idea quickly became popular with the remaining states. It wasn't until February 6, 1788 that Massachusetts ratified the Constitution, but not until it had exacted a promise that a subsequent Amendment process would in fact provide a Bill of Rights. The remaining states followed Massachusetts lead and ratified with the same promise. It is truly ironic that while Massachusetts was the prime mover for a Bill of Rights in 1788, today Massachusetts has all but eliminated the right to bear arms.

On June 21, 1788 New Hampshire became the ninth state to ratify the Constitution, thereby making it the supreme law of the land. James Madison, true to his promise, introduced a Bill of Rights to the first Congress. On September 25, 1789 that first Congress adopted the Bill of Rights and sent them to the states for ratification.

It should be noted the original Bill of Rights contained twelve Amendments of which only ten were ratified by the necessary three-fourths of the States. Today those first Ten Amendments are known as the Bill of Rights. Only the first eight amendments contain individual rights. The ninth and tenth amendments reaffirm the sovereignty of the states.

Amendment I

Congress shall make no law respecting an establishment of religion, or prohibiting the free exercise thereof; or abridging the freedom of speech, or of the press; or the right of the people peaceably to assemble, and to petition the Government for a redress of grievances.

The first Amendment identifies five rights on our grocery list. When the original colonies declared their independence from England it was common practice for Kings to recognize a state religion to the point of preventing and suppression of others. The first right is simply (congress) shall not establish a state religion. The second right, Congress is not to prohibit the free exercise thereof. Remember the Constitution is about things the federal government cannot do. Therefore, Congress cannot prevent a sovereign state from incorporating religion in their activities. A local school that wants to recite the Lord's Prayer before the start of school every day is well within its Constitutional right. In the Constitution, a religious right is equally on par with civil rights. In Federalists 51 Madison had the following to say, "In a free government the security for civil rights must be the same as that for religious rights." If the States want to establish a state religion it is not unconstitutional to do so. As a matter of fact at the time of ratification for the Bill of Rights, Massachusetts, Connecticut and New Hampshire retained their colonial religious establishments.[40]

The case of Barrow county Georgia in July of 2006 that forced a local courthouse to remove a display of the Ten Commandments from its walls is clearly unconstitutional. The Supreme Court has dictated to a local community that they

---

[40] See Appendix: Thomas Jefferson

cannot display the Ten Commandments because of religious overtones. The first amendment gives no such authority to congress or the Judiciary to dictate how a local community wants to run its religious affairs. The first amendment does not eliminate religion from the public square; it gives freedom to the people to determine their own destiny in those matters. A single individual with the support of the ACLU has usurped the will of the people. The beauty of our Constitution and concept of Sovereign States is the ability of each state to set their morals and standards and if as an individual you do not like it then you have the right to chose by moving to a place that is more in tune to your beliefs. The old Soviet Union practiced central planning; now it looks like our Congressmen are in the same habit.

The third and fourth rights in this Amendment are the freedom of speech and the freedom of press. Too often people confuse the freedom to speak with a right to speak. You have a right to speak without interference from the government, but you do not have a right to force others to support it. For example, many times an athlete will make a slanderous or hostile statement and the league or team will punish him for speaking out. Yes he has a right to speak, in other words the government cannot prevent his speech, however, on the other hand he has no right to force others to pay for his forum. He has no right to expect his boss, the team owner, to continue to pay him if he chooses to make inflammatory public statements that his boss may disagree with.

Another example, often seen on college campuses, is when a person is physically removed from a public hall where someone is lecturing because he is heckling or otherwise interrupting the speaker. Those in attendance are often the first to cry the freedom of speech mantra. Yes, but whoever, paid for that microphone and the hall has no obligation to allow the individual to speak. That individual does, however, have the right to purchase his own auditorium and microphone and speak to anyone who wishes to attend. One of my favorite pundits and economists, Walter E. Williams has defined a right as, "...something that exists simultaneously among people...but confers no obligation on another."

The last clause gives the people the right to peaceably assemble and offer redress to the government. Yes you will probably need to obtain a permit for the public assembly, but that only helps the local authorities determine if and to what degree security might be necessary. Your only beef here is if your permit is denied.

Amendment II

A well regulated Militia, being necessary to the security of a free State, the right of the people to keep and bear arms, shall not be infringed.

Keep the following in mind, the Constitution and the Bill of Rights are not rights conferred to us by government, they are instead, the recognition of unalienable rights by our creator that the government cannot and must not extinguish. Lawyers love to obfuscate this Amendment, but it is one of the easiest to understand. As we continue down our grocery list we pick up two more rights in the second amendment. One: the right to a well regulated Militia and two: the right of the people to keep and bear arms. The second sentence, 'being necessary to the security of a free state,' is a parenthetical expression defining the reason for a well regulated Militia. Case closed!

Amendment III

No Soldier shall, in time of peace be quartered in any house, without the consent of the Owner, nor in time of war, but in a manner to be prescribed by law.

At the time of our founding, large military bases that housed soldiers were unheard of. This amendment was to protect the property rights of citizens. Property rights and personal rights are the linchpin of our freedoms guaranteed by the Constitution; both of which are under a relentless assault by my and your congressman.

Amendment IV

The right of the people to be secure in their persons, houses, papers, and effects, against unreasonable searches and seizures, shall not be violated, and no Warrants shall issue, but upon probable cause, supported by Oath or affirmation, and particularly describing the place to be searched, and the persons or things to be seized.

The great American experiment was founded on the basic principle of property rights strengthened by self-reliant, rugged, individualism. As we continue our shopping spree, the fourth amendment identifies yet another right. The government cannot simply charge into anyone's property without a search warrant issued by a judge. Furthermore, to obtain that warrant there must be sufficient and probable cause before a judge is to issue same. This applies to criminal law only, in other words it does not give the tax assessor in your town the right to periodically come into your home and inspect it.

Amendment V

No person shall be held to answer for a capital, or otherwise infamous crime, unless on a presentment or indictment of a Grand Jury, except in cases arising in the land or naval forces, or in the Militia, when in actual service in time of War or public danger; nor shall any person be subject for the same offense to be twice put in jeopardy of life or limb; nor shall be compelled in any criminal case to be a witness against himself, nor be deprived of life, liberty, or property, without due process of law; nor shall private property be taken for public use, without just compensation.

Only half way through and our shopping cart is getting quite full. The Fifth Amendment recognizes six more rights. One, before a person can be charged with a capital or other infamous crime the government must first present evidence to and get an indictment from a Grand Jury. Two, the exception to one above is in the case of war where we saw in Article I, Section 8, Clause 14 military tribunals are both necessary and Constitutional. Three, once a person is acquitted or found innocent he cannot be charged again for the same offense. Four, no one is required to testify or be a witness against themself. This is where we get the phrase, "I take the fifth Amendment." Five, as recognized in the Declaration of Independence our unalienable right to life, liberty and the pursuit of happiness cannot be taken from us without due process of law. Six, as discussed in Article I, Section 8, Clause 19 the government can take land for public use but must pay just compensation which means, they must pay market price for property taken. It does not allow government to take land from one person and give to another person as in the Kelo v. New London, Connecticut case of 2005.

Amendment VI

In all criminal prosecutions, the accused shall enjoy the right to a speedy and public trial, by an impartial jury of the State and district wherein the crime shall have been committed, which districts shall have been previously ascertained by law, and to be informed of the nature and cause of the accusation; to be confronted with the witnesses against him; to have compulsory process for obtaining witnesses in his favor, and to have the Assistance of Counsel for his defence.

This Amendment recognizes yet five more rights. One, in cases of criminal prosecutions the accused cannot be incarcerated indefinitely but must be given a speedy trial. Two, the accused has the right to an impartial jury in the district where the crime shall have been committed. Three, the accused has the right to be informed of the nature of the accusation. Four, the accused has the right to be confronted with witnesses against him and to have witnesses in his favor when they exist. Five, all defendants have a right to counsel; even if the accused cannot afford an attorney the funds must come from the public treasurer.

Amendment VII

In Suits at common law, where the value in controversy shall exceed twenty dollars, the right of trial by jury shall be preserved, and no fact tried by a jury, shall be otherwise re-examined in any Court of the United States, than according to the rules of the common law.

Protects the right of trial by jury in civil cases.

Amendment VIII

Excessive bail shall not be required, nor excessive fines imposed, nor cruel and unusual punishments inflicted.
If you are charged with stealing a pair of sneakers a million dollar bail would be considered excessive, likewise a million dollar fine for stealing the sneakers would also be an excessive fine. Cruel and unusual punishment would be the removal of a hand for stealing the sneakers. On the other hand, no pun intended, the death penalty is not cruel or unusual punishment for premeditated murder. Although our shopping cart is full on this trip, we can come back for more for our rights do not end here.

Amendment IX

The enumeration in the Constitution, of certain rights, shall not be construed to deny or disparage others retained by the people.
Many have stated there is no substantive difference between the ninth and tenth Amendments. Our forefathers, on the other hand, understood clearly the difference between a right and a power. To that end the ninth Amendment is, once again, about individual and unalienable rights while the tenth is about power to the federal government and state sovereignty.

The founders feared that listing the rights expressed in the Bill of Rights would be taken as the only rights held by the citizens. The ninth Amendment clearly addresses that issue. Although some basic rights of the people were spelled out in this Bill of Rights it is understood these were not finite in scope. Anything not specifically stated in the Constitution or Article

I, section 8, was left solely to the individual states. Once again we see the doctrine of "When in doubt, the States win-out."

Amendment X

The powers not delegated to the United States by the Constitution, nor prohibited by it to the States, are reserved to the States respectively, or to the people.

State Sovereignty, the tenth amendment assures that the federal government will only exercise the enumerated powers.[41] "The powers delegated by the proposed Constitution to the Federal government are few and defined. Those which are to remain in the state governments are numerous and indefinite."[42]

In Federalist 21, Alexander Hamilton had the following to say about state rights, "That each State shall retain every power, jurisdiction, and right, not EXPRESSLY delegated to the United States in Congress assembled. There is, doubtless, a striking absurdity in supposing that a right of this kind does not exist." In other words, *"When in doubt, the states win out."*

---

[41] Refer to Article I, Section 8
[42] James Madison, Federalists 45

Chapter 10

Amendment XI   Ratified February 7, 1795 (340 days)

State Sovereignty.

The Judicial power of the United States shall not be construed to extend to any suit in law or equity, commenced or prosecuted against one of the United States by Citizens of another State, or by Citizens or Subjects of any Foreign State.

This amendment is also about state sovereignty. It simply means the federal courts would be limited to those items in Article III. Recall Section 2, gave the federal courts jurisdiction in suits, "...between a State and Citizens of another State...and between a State, or the Citizens thereof, and foreign States, Citizens or Subjects." The states did not like the idea that the federal government would sit in judgment of suits brought about from state to state or citizen to a state. In other words if an individual brought a suit against a sovereign state the states felt it a threat to their sovereignty having the federal

84

government meddling. The eleventh Amendment simply banned the initiation of suits against states in the federal courts. In other words this Amendment establishes the separation of powers between state courts and Federal courts.

Alexander Hamilton speaks directly to state sovereignty when he says, "It is inherent in the nature of sovereignty not to be amenable to the suit of an individual WITHOUT ITS CONSENT. This is the general sense, and the general practice of mankind; and the exemption, as one of the attributes of sovereignty, is now enjoyed by the government of every State in the Union."[43]

For example, if a citizen of New Hampshire wants to sue the state of Massachusetts or his own state government, the federal government has no say in the matter; however, as a general rule, no state will allow its citizens or citizens of other states to sue it. that is what is meant by "WITHOUT ITS CONSENT" in the above quote from Hamilton. Keep in mind, though, the Constitution does give us, the citizens, the right to hold both our state and federal governments accountable to our rights under the Constitution. A state that forbids a law-abiding citizen from owning a hand gun can be sued. No, you cannot sue the state because a pot-hole destroyed the front end of your automobile.

Amendment XII   Ratified June 15, 1804 (189 days)

Article II, Section 1, Clause 3 established the means of choosing the President and Vice President. Amendment XII changes those procedures.

The Electors shall meet in their respective states, and vote by ballot for President and Vice President, one of

---

[43] Hamilton, Federalists 81

whom, at least, shall not be an inhabitant of the same state with themselves;

In the first sentence of Article II, Section 1, Clause 3 the Electors were voting for President only and the second place vote getter would be Vice President. The first sentence of the Twelfth Amendment has the Electors voting for the ticket of President and Vice President. Why this nuanced difference you may ask? The framers did not envision the advent of political parties. Therefore, when in the election of 1800 the first known ticket for President and Vice President was introduced in the party of Jefferson and Burr, each Elector voted in the manner established in Article II, Section 1, Clause 3. Jefferson received a majority of votes for President, but because Burr was on the same ballot with Jefferson he got the same number of votes as Jefferson. Everyone knew what they meant, but the manner of the wording in Article II sent the election to the House of Representatives. The Twelfth Amendment ratified four years later avoided the unintended consequences when the first sentence was changed to read a vote for President and Vice President. They kept the requirement that both candidates could not be from the same state. The second sentence in this clause says;

…they shall name in their ballots the person voted for as President, and in distinct ballots the person voted for as Vice-President, and they shall make distinct lists of all persons voted for as President, and of all persons voted for as Vice-President and of the number of votes for each, which lists they shall sign and certify, and transmit sealed to the seat of the government of the United States, directed to the President of the Senate;

A list of whom they voted for shall be signed and certified then forwarded to the President of the Senate. Similar to Article II, except here they actually name a President and Vice President.

- the President of the Senate shall, in the presence of the Senate and House of Representatives, open all the certificates and the votes shall then be counted; - The person having the greatest number of votes for President, shall be the President, if such number be a majority of the whole number of Electors appointed;

The first part of this sentence clarifies once again that the Electors are voting for President and Vice President; the remainder is the same as Article II which says, after casting their votes they shall make a list of all the persons they voted for and the number of votes each one received. They shall then certify the votes and send them to the President of the Senate. Once all the votes are received the President of the Senate shall, in the presents of both houses of Congress, open and tally the votes.

The person with the greatest number of votes shall be President, if that number is a majority. Note, a majority need not be 51% if there is a third party involved as we saw in the William Clinton, Bob Dole, Ross Perot election of 1996. Clinton received 49%, Dole received 41% and Ross Perot received 8%; Although, Clinton won by less than 51% he received the greatest number of votes in what is said to be a plurality because there were more than two candidates.

and if no person have such majority, then from the persons having the highest numbers not exceeding three on the list of those voted for as President, the House of

87

Representatives shall choose immediately, by ballot, the President.

If there is a tie or no clear majority, the House must choose the President. Since Jefferson and Burr no other election has gone to the House. A scenario in which that could happen would be the following: say for example, there were five major parties running for President and each of them received in the neighborhood of 20%. This situation would require the House to choose a President from the top three vote getters. However, our present two party system renders this a highly unlikely scenario.

But in choosing the President, the votes shall be taken by states, the representation from each state having one vote; a quorum for this purpose shall consist of a member or members from two-thirds of the states, and a majority of all the states shall be necessary to a choice.

Nothing changed here from Article II. Before the House can vote there must be a quorum of two-thirds of the States. The quorum needed is defined as at least one Representative from two-thirds of the states. The elections then would proceed with only a majority of the states needed to elect.

And if the House of Representatives shall not choose a President whenever the right of choice shall devolve upon them, before the fourth day of March next following, then the Vice-President shall act as President, as in the case of the death or other constitutional disability of the President.[44]

At the time of the Twelfth Amendment the inauguration of a new President took place on March 4 which required the House to make their choice prior to that date. If for some reason they could not make their choice in that time frame the

---

[44] Changed by Section 3 of the Twentieth Amendment.

Vice-President would become President until such election by the House was complete. This clause will be changed again by the twentieth Amendment.

The person having the greatest number of votes as Vice-President, shall be the Vice-President, if such number be a majority of the whole number of Electors appointed,

The Vice President, like the President shall carry a majority of the Electors to be elected.

and if no person have a majority, then from the two highest numbers on the list, the Senate shall choose the Vice-President;

If there is no majority the Senate shall choose from the highest two vote getters.

a quorum for the purpose shall consist of two-thirds of the whole number of Senators,

As in the House for there to be a quorum in the Senate two-thirds of them shall be present.**and a majority of the whole number shall be necessary to a choice.**

Only a majority is necessary to chose the Vice President.

But no person constitutionally ineligible to the office of President shall be eligible to that of Vice-President of the United States.

The Vice President must have the same Constitutional requirement as President.

Amendment XIII   Ratified December 6, 1865 (309 days)

Section 1:

Neither slavery nor involuntary servitude, except as a punishment for crime whereof the party shall have been

duly convicted, shall exist within the United States, or any place subject to their jurisdiction.

Eliminates clause 3, section 2, Article IV. Abolishes slavery; and no gentleman the draft for military service is not slavery.

Section 2:

Congress shall have power to enforce this article by appropriate legislation.

Self evident, congress can enforce through legislation.

Amendment XIV   Ratified July 9, 1868 (757 days)

Section 1:

All persons born or naturalized in the United States, and subject to the jurisdiction thereof, are citizens of the United States and of the State wherein they reside. No State shall make or enforce any law which shall abridge the privileges or immunities of citizens of the United States; nor shall any State deprive any person of life, liberty, or property, without due process of law; nor deny to any person within its jurisdiction the equal protection of the laws.

We just saw the thirteenth Amendment abolish slavery. However, white southerners were intent on regaining power over the former black slaves. To do this, many if not all southern states, created Black Codes, which served to inhibit the freedom of ex-slaves. These codes included state laws that regulated ex-slave rights, to include marriage, freedom of speech, freedom of movement and the right to hold and sell property. They even dictated the types of employment allowed such as agricultural workers or domestic labor jobs. Black codes went so far as to prevent them from self-sufficiency by raising their own crops. As if these procedures weren't prohibitive enough, they would also be arrested and jailed as vagrants if found to be unemployed.

In response to the Black Codes Congress quickly introduced the fourteenth Amendment to ensure that all former slaves were granted automatic United States citizenship, and that they would have all the rights and privileges as any other citizen. Some, lawyers, have questioned the validity of the fourteenth Amendment because the southern states had succeeded from the union as a result of the Civil War, and they were not allowed re-admittance to the Union until they ratified the fourteenth Amendment. That line of thought is absolute nonsense. A requirement for membership has been a characteristic of mankind throughout history. If one wishes to join a choir, knowing how to sing is a prerequisite. Regardless of the organization there are requirements of membership. To become part of the United States of America after the Civil War required one to subscribe to its Constitution and Amendments.

Section 2:

Representatives shall be apportioned among the several States according to their respective numbers, counting the whole number of persons in each State, excluding Indians not taxed. But when the right to vote at any election for the choice of electors for President and Vice-President of the United States, Representatives in Congress, the Executive and Judicial officers of a State, or the members of the Legislature thereof, is denied to any of the male inhabitants of such State, being twenty-one years of age,[45] and citizens of the United States, or in any way abridged, except for

---

[45] Changed by section 1 of the Twenty-Sixth Amendment

participation in rebellion, or other crime, the basis of representation therein shall be reduced in the proportion which the number of such male citizens shall bear to the whole number of male citizens twenty-one years of age in such State.

Article I, section 2 established the number of Representatives by counting all free men and three-fifths of slaves. Section 2, of the fourteenth Amendment erases the three-fifths slave requirement and gives all free males twenty one years of age or older the right to vote and be counted for representation.

Section 3:

No person shall be a Senator or Representative in Congress, or elector of President and Vice-President, or hold any office, civil or military, under the United States, or under any State, who, having previously taken an oath, as a member of Congress, or as an officer of the United States, or as a member of any State legislature, or as an executive or judicial officer of any State, to support the Constitution of the United States, shall have engaged in insurrection or rebellion against the same, or given aid or comfort to the enemies thereof. But Congress may by vote of two-thirds of each House, remove such disability.

In the wake of reconstruction after the Civil War the southern states that had seceded from the Union were considered to have partaken in a rebellion against the United States. After re-admittance to the Union this clause was placed in the Amendment to aid and allow those from southern states access to the political process of the United States.

Section 4:

The validity of the public debt of the United States, authorized by law, including debts incurred for payment of pensions and bounties for services in suppressing insurrection or rebellion, shall not be questioned. But neither the United States nor any State shall assume or pay any debt or obligation incurred in aid of insurrection or rebellion against the United States, or any claim for the loss or emancipation of any slave; but all such debts, obligations and claims shall be held illegal and void.

This section simply says the public debt of the United States, authorized by law, including those incurred as a result of the Revolution will not be questioned. It also states that any monies claimed as a lost, be they real or imagined, as a result of the thirteenth Amendment (emancipation of slaves) will be illegal and void. Enough time has passed now that this Amendment is pretty much a moot issue. What it boils down to is the South had to help pay for the war but could make no monetary claims because of the war or the emancipation of slaves.

Section 5:

The Congress shall have power to enforce, by appropriate legislation, the provisions of this article.

Congress has the power to enact laws to enforce this article.

Amendment XV   Ratified February 3, 1870 (342 days)

Section 1:

The right of citizens of the United States to vote shall not be denied or abridged by the United States or by any

State on account of race, color, or previous condition of servitude.

The thirteenth, fourteenth and fifteenth Amendments were known as the Reconstruction Amendments. The last of these, the fifteenth, was designed to close the last loophole in the establishment of civil rights for newly-freed black slaves. It simply states that a person's race, color, or prior history as a slave could not be used to prevent them from voting or exercising other rights of citizenship.

Section 2:

The Congress shall have power to enforce this article by appropriate legislation.

Congress has the power to enact laws to enforce this article.

Amendment XVI   Ratified February 3, 1913 (1,302 days)

The Congress shall have power to lay and collect taxes on incomes, from whatever source derived, without apportionment among the several States, and without regard to any census or enumeration.

This Amendment establishes the personal income tax and the much beloved IRS. It changes Article I, Section 9, Clause 4. From that day on we were assured by our Congressman the tax would never exceed three percent and would only apply to the upper level of incomes. This Amendment went a long way in teaching our Congressmen they could lie to us and we would believe it. This reminds me of the two farmers who were talking; one said to the other, "How can you tell if a politician is lying?" "His lips are moving," said the other.

Amendment XVII   Ratified April 8, 1913 (330 days)

The Senate of the United States shall be composed of two Senators from each State, elected by the people thereof, for six years; and each Senator shall have one vote. The electors in each State shall have the qualifications requisite for electors of the most numerous branch of the State legislatures.

In Article I, section 3, the Senators were chosen by state legislatures. The first clause of this Amendment sends the election of Senators to the people of each state.

When vacancies happen in the representation of any State in the Senate, the executive authority of such State shall issue writs of election to fill such vacancies: Provided, That the legislature of any State may empower the executive thereof to make temporary appointments until the people fill the vacancies by election as the legislature may direct.

This clause also modifies Article I, section 3. It says if there is a vacancy of a U.S. Senate seat the Governor of that state may appoint his replacement; although, the power of the Governor to appoint must have first been established by the state legislature. Any state governor lacking this legislative authority must fill the vacancy by a special election as directed by the state legislature.

This amendment shall not be so construed as to affect the election or term of any Senator chosen before it becomes valid as part of the Constitution.

The ratification of this amendment will not be ex post facto. In other words it will not affect any Senator prior to its ratification but will be applicable from the date of ratification forward.

Amendment XVIII   Ratified January 16, 1919 (394 days)

Section 1:

After one year from the ratification of this article the manufacture, sale, or transportation of intoxicating liquors within, the importation thereof into, or the exportation thereof from the United States and all territory subject to the jurisdiction thereof for beverage purposes is hereby prohibited.[46]

Some say the "Women's War" of 1873-74 was the precursor to this amendment, but whatever the reason the eighteenth Amendment outlawed Alcohol.   It is interesting to note that after ratification it would not go into effect for one year. Perhaps that was to give everyone time to establish alternative methods of procuring alcohol.

Section 2:

The Congress and the several States shall have concurrent power to enforce this article by appropriate legislation.

Probably recognizing the difficulty of enforcing this amendment, Congress gave authority to the states as well as Congress to enact laws necessary to enforce prohibition.

Section 3:

This article shall be inoperative unless it shall have been ratified as an amendment to the Constitution by the legislatures of the several States, as provided in the Constitution, within seven years from the date of the submission hereof to the States by the Congress.

---

[46] Repealed by the Twenty-First Amendment

The states had seven years to ratify the amendment.

Amendment XIX   Ratified August 18, 1920 (441 days)

The right of citizens of the United States to vote shall not be denied or abridged by the United States or by any State on account of sex. Congress shall have power to enforce this article by appropriate legislation.

Women's suffrage, gives women the right to vote. Perhaps after the so called "Women's War" and their apparent temperance victory they thought it was time to strike and gain the right to vote. One day they will probably want to be President.

Amendment XX   Ratified January 23, 1933 (327 days)

Section 1:

The terms of the President and Vice President shall end at noon on the 20th day of January, and the terms of Senators and Representatives at noon on the 3rd day of January, of the years in which such terms would have ended if this article had not been ratified; and the terms of their successors shall then begin.

This clause establishes the terms of office for President, Vice President, Senators and Representatives.

Section 2:

The Congress shall assemble at least once in every year, and such meeting shall begin at noon on the 3rd day of January, unless they shall by law appoint a different day.

Article I, section 4, established the first Monday in December as the date for Congress to assemble; this clause moves that date to the third day of January each year. The date, however, can be changed by law. Typically, prior to the close of a session, congress will set a date for reassembly in January. Congress has met every January since 1933 but not always on the third.

Section 3:

If, at the time fixed for the beginning of the term of the President, the President elect shall have died, the Vice President elect shall become President. If a President shall not have been chosen before the time fixed for the beginning of his term, or if the President elect shall have failed to qualify, then the Vice President elect shall act as President until a President shall have qualified; and the Congress may by law provide for the case wherein neither a President elect nor a Vice President elect shall have qualified, declaring who shall then act as President, or the manner in which one who is to act shall be selected, and such person shall act accordingly until a President or Vice President shall have qualified.

Contrary to all the baloney mine and your congressman spew about having no authority to investigate the Constitutional eligibility of a President or Vice President, the twentieth amendment specifically states if the President or President elect shall fail the Constitutional requirements for his office then the Vice President or Vice President elect shall become President, provided he meets the Constitutional requirements for office.

Section 4:

The Congress may by law provide for the case of the death of any of the persons from whom the House of Representatives may choose a President whenever the right of choice shall have devolved upon them, and for the case of

the death of any of the persons from whom the Senate may choose a Vice President whenever the right of choice shall have devolved upon them.

In the unlikely event the election of President and Vice President should devolve to the House of Representative and the Senate respectively and either or both of them should die before assuming office, the Senate shall decide what the succession shall be.

Section 5:

Sections 1 and 2 shall take effect on the 15th day of October following the ratification of this article.

If ratified this Amendment will become effective on the 15th of October next.

Section 6:

This article shall be inoperative unless it shall have been ratified as an amendment to the Constitution by the legislatures of three-fourth of the several States within seven years from the date of its submission.

A seven year dead line date for ratification.

Amendment XXI   Ratified December 5, 1933 (288 days)

Section 1:

The eighteenth article of amendment to the Constitution of the United States is hereby repealed.

This is the only Amendment to repeal another.

Section 2:

The transportation or importation into any State, Territory, or possession of the United States for delivery or use therein of intoxicating liquors, in violation of the laws thereof, is hereby prohibited.

Although prohibition is repealed each state has the authority to regulate alcohol within its borders.

Section 3:

The article shall be inoperative unless it shall have been ratified as an amendment to the Constitution by conventions in the several States, as provided in the Constitution, within seven years from the date of the submission hereof to the States by the Congress.

If not ratified within seven years the Amendment would be null and void. It is interesting to note, only the Twelfth, Twenty-Third and Twenty-Sixth Amendments were ratified faster than the Twenty-First.

Amendment XXII   Ratified February 27, 1951 (1,439 days)

Section 1:

No person shall be elected to the office of the President more than twice, and no person who has held the office of President, or acted as President, for more than two years of a term to which some other person was elected President shall be elected to the office of the President more than once. But this Article shall not apply to any person holding the office of President, when this Article was proposed by the Congress, and shall not prevent any person who may

be holding the office of President, or acting as President, during the term within which this Article becomes operative from holding the office of President or acting as President, during the remainder of such term.

Sets term limits for the President. Two terms and you are out. The only exception is if as Vice President you took office with less than two years then you can still run for two terms. But if you took over with two years or more then you only get one more term.

Section 2:

This article shall be inoperative unless it shall have been ratified as an amendment to the Constitution by the legislatures of three-fourths of the several States within seven years from the date of its submission to the States by the Congress.

The states had seven years to approve it.

Amendment XXIII   Ratified March 29, 1961 (285 days)

Section 1:

The District constituting the seat of Government of the United States shall appoint in such manner as the Congress may direct:

A number of electors of President and Vice President equal to the whole number of Senators and Representatives in Congress to which the District would be entitled if it were a State, but in no event more than the least populous State; they shall be in addition to those appointed by the States, but they shall be considered, for the purposes of the election of President and Vice President, to be electors appointed by

a State; and they shall meet in the District and perform such duties as provided by the twelfth article of amendment.

This Amendment gives residents of the Federal District of Columbia the right to vote in Presidential Elections. Although, I am not opposed to this in General and one might guess no one is opposed to this Amendment it sure gives one cause to be concerned. Why, well it is the beginning of a Government who thinks it their job to make things "fair". Worse yet it puts government in the position of determining what is fair. People make choices in life; upon moving to DC before this Amendment one knew the conditions. If voting in the Presidential elections were important to you there were plenty of places in the surrounding states to move. The District we are talking about is only ten square miles. Living outside the District in a surrounding state so that you have a right to vote and commuting to work is not a terribly demanding proposition. There are many cities in America with a larger population and longer commute.

An imposition, probably, but again it is a choice; the more important thing to me would be the preservation of the uniqueness of our Constitution. But as stated earlier I am not necessarily opposed to it, especially since there are many more important unconstitutional happenings since this amendment that we need to concentrate on. Perhaps my larger point here is to be wary of anyone desirous to change the Constitution to make things fair. The Constitution as it stands today is the ultimate document of fairness, because it allows everyone the right to choose

Amendments like these are what I call feel good amendments. No one is really opposed to them, but they are introduced as a diversion to keep American citizens focus away from the bigger picture. There has been talk of introducing a flag amendment, to prevent the desecration of the American flag. Although, most, myself included, would not be opposed to such an amendment, it is nothing more than a feel good amendment to keep the American public's attention away from the numerous amendments and Constitutional provisions that are presently being trampled by the same congress who want to float a flag amendment. When these people learn to live by the Constitution and Amendments we all ready have then perhaps we can consider new amendments.

Section 2:

The Congress shall have power to enforce this article by appropriate legislation.

Congress has the power to enact laws to enforce this article.

Amendment XXIV   Ratified January 23, 1964 (514 days)

Section 1:

The right of citizens of the United States to vote in any primary or other election for President or Vice President, for electors for President or Vice President, or for Senator or Representative in Congress, shall not be denied or abridged by the United States or any State by reason of failure to pay any poll tax or other tax.

During the early history of our nation, the original thirteen colonies, the first thirteen states and subsequent states since then up to the early sixties imposed a variety of pole tax. The tax was generally small but served to keep the poorer community members from voting. After all it was argued those with a financial interest should be the ones to vote.

Prior to the Civil War the pole tax had dwindled to nearly nonexistent; however, after the Reconstruction Amendments we visited above (13, 14, and 15) the pole tax gained in popularity again in the South as an attempt to keep the Blacks from voting. Although, many court cases were fought over this it wasn't until the ratification of the Twenty-Fourth Amendment that eliminated any kind of tax as a prerequisite to vote. Yes, you can owe the IRS thousands of dollars and still vote. Provided, of course, you aren't in jail.

Section 2:

The Congress shall have power to enforce this article by appropriate legislation.

Congress has the power to enact laws to enforce this article.

Amendment XXV   Ratified February 10, 1967 (584 days)

Section 1:

In case of the removal of the President from office or of his death or resignation, the Vice President shall become President.

Replaces and clarifies Article II, Section 1, Clause 7 by designating the Vice President as President in the event of his removal, resignation or death.

Section 2:

Whenever there is a vacancy in the office of the Vice President, the President shall nominate a Vice President

who shall take office upon confirmation by a majority vote of both Houses of Congress.

On October 10, 1973 Spiro T. Agnew resigned the Vice Presidency. The President, Richard M. Nixon, nominated the House Republican leader Gerald R. Ford who was confirmed by both houses of Congress. This was the first such appointment made under the Twenty-Fifth Amendment. Less than one year later in August, 1974 President Nixon was forced to resign. Then Vice President Ford becomes President and invokes the Twenty-Fifth Amendment to appoint New York Governor Nelson Rockefeller as Vice President. This was the first time in American history that neither the President nor the Vice President was elected by the people.

Section 3:

Whenever the President transmits to the President pro tempore of the Senate and the Speaker of the House of Representatives his written declaration that he is unable to discharge the powers and duties of his office, and until he transmits to them a written declaration to the contrary, such powers and duties shall be discharged by the Vice President as Acting President.

Unfortunately the assassination of President Kennedy in 1963 not only shocked and saddened a nation but exposed a circumstance not covered by the Constitution. After the tragedy it was speculated that if Kennedy were to survive, because of the modern advancements of medicine, it was surmised that he might, if he did live he would still be President but in a coma. This condition left a power vacuum in the government. The third clause of this Amendment addresses that concern.

This section of the Twenty-Fifth Amendment has never been invoked, although it came perilously close during the assassination attempt on March 30, 1981 of President Ronald Reagan. Aides were worried that relinquishing power, even temporarily, would tarnish Reagan's image. His counselor Edwin Meese later said, "...there was a real concern not to provide any appearance of a President unable to continue to run the country." What led Meese to this decision was the Presidents consciousness before, during and after the attempt. The President even joked with his Wife while being transported to the Hospital that he forgot to duck. While at the Hospital he asked if the Doctors were Republicans.

Although the provisions of the Twenty-Fifth Amendment were in place, Reagan's practice of delegating responsibilities served him well in the weeks after the shooting. Reagan never faltered. His courage and leadership were sound, solid and on display for the country and world. The Twenty-Fifth Amendment was never invoked.

Section 4:

Whenever the Vice President and a majority of either the principal officers of the executive departments or of such other body as Congress may by law provide, transmit to the President pro tempore of the Senate and the Speaker of the House of Representatives their written declaration that the President is unable to discharge the powers and duties of his office, the Vice President shall immediately assume the powers and duties of the office as Acting president.

In 1787 Pennsylvania Representative John Dickinson asked, "What is the extent of the term 'disability,' and who is to be the judge of it?" With President Dwight Eisenhower's Heart attack in 1955, an abdominal operation in 1956 and a subsequent stroke in 1957 and nuclear arms proliferation growing among the Super Powers, Congress realized a pressing need to define 'disability.' The burden of proof is obviously and necessarily high, however, if the Vice President and the President's Cabinet can, as a unit, present to the President pro tempore of the Senate and the Speaker of the House of Representatives a written declaration that the President is unable to discharge the powers and duties of his office the Vice President shall immediately assume the office as Acting President.

Thereafter, when the President transmits to the President pro tempore of the Senate and the Speaker of the House of Representatives his written declaration that no inability exists, he shall resume the powers and duties of his office

When said disability is removed the President must transmit to the President pro tempore and the Speaker of the House of Representatives the inability no longer exist.

unless the Vice President and a majority of either the principal officers of the executive department or of such other body as Congress may by law provide, transmit within four days to the President pro tempore of the Senate and the Speaker of the House of Representatives their written declaration that the President is unable to discharge the powers and duties of his office.

If, on the other hand, the Vice President and cabinet continue to disagree with the President they must transmit to same within four days.

Thereupon Congress shall decide the issue, assembling within forty-eight hours for that purpose if not in session.

If the Congress, within twenty-one days after receipt of the latter written declaration, or, if Congress is not in session, within twenty-one days after Congress is required to assemble, determines by two-thirds vote of both Houses that the President is unable to discharge the powers and duties of his office, the Vice President shall continue to discharge the same as Acting President; otherwise, the President shall resume the powers and duties of his office.

Congress must then decide this issue by a two-thirds majority of both Houses. If Congress fails to act within twenty-one days the President shall resume the powers and duties of his office.

Amendment XXVI   Ratified July 1, 1971 (100 days)

Section 1:

The right of citizens of the United States, who are eighteen years of age or older, to vote shall not be denied or abridged by the United States or by any State on account of age.

Reduces the voting age from 21 in section 2, Amendment XIV to 18; conservatives never knew what hit them with this one. At the beginning of this book it was remarked that the Constitution is synonymous with Conservativism. Conservatism is embodied in a rational thought process. The liberalism of the 60's continuing today is based on emotion. Emotions by definition are easily refuted by rational thought. By gaining the eighteen year old vote liberals acquired a large voting bloc. The eighteen to twenty year old has not gained the life experience and reasoning powers necessary for rational discussion, he is still guided by emotion. Just mention buzz words like, 'fair,' 'rights,' 'the rich,' 'minimum wage,' 'greedy corporations,' 'the poor,' and many more then watch the liberal swoon with mightier than thou delight; never a coherent thought on these topics. If you have read this far without buyer's remorse, congratulations you're on the right side of the Constitution.

This reminds me of the old worn out argument by the feel good left that an eighteen year old who fights and dies for his country should be allowed to consume alcohol. This is a typical feel good position by the left. For when put to the test it is nothing more than an apples to oranges comparison. The eighteen year old soldier is trained for eight hours a day for a minimum of eight weeks. He is told when to load his weapon, when to point it, when to pull the trigger, when to stop, when to unload it, when to store it. That same eighteen year old in a bar has no such individual instructing him as to when it is safe to start drinking and when it is time to stop.

No one would turn an eighteen year old loose on the battlefield with a loaded weapon without sufficient training and guidance. Why then would we want an eighteen year old turned loose in a bar without the benefit of wisdom that comes with a more mature age?

Section 2:

The Congress shall have power to enforce this article by appropriate legislation.

Congress has the power to enact laws to enforce this article.

Amendment XXVII   Ratified May 7, 1992 (74,003 days)

That is not a misprint; it took more than 200 years to ratify this Amendment. Real decision makers we have, but they never miss a chance at a pay raise.

No law varying the compensation for the services of the Senators and Representatives shall take effect, until an election of Representatives shall have intervened.

Congress can vote themselves a raise but must wait until at least one election cycle of the House of Representatives before it takes effect. While we are in the midst of one of the greatest economic melt downs since the great depression Congress has given them self a raise. Now Obama did say prior to his inauguration that everyone would, "Have some skin in the game," when it came to belt tightening in this economy; Oh! He didn't mean the 535 members of Congress.

CHAPTER 11

CONCLUSION

There you have it, the Constitution at its simplest and most basic meaning. There is an old adage in education, origin unknown, which goes something like this, "If you don't know your subject make it difficult." Any lawyer, congressman or judge who tells you the Constitution is difficult and its true deep meaning can only be determined by them is only practicing obfuscation by making the subject difficult. They simply do not understand the subject. They are trying to create fear of the Constitution in order to control us.

In order that we may take our country back we must first stop treating our politicians as rock stars. Next we must stop thinking that the problem is with all other congressmen and not ours. Perhaps we could accomplish this latter task by simply asking the potential vote seeker if he will sign on to and pass H.R.1359 the Enumerated Powers Act, which will require Congress to specify the source of authority under the United States Constitution for the enactment of laws, and for other purposes. Perhaps then, they will become the child in the crowd who is seen but not heard. Let us not forget, our politicians work for us, not the other way around, we get to set the rules of employment. If you do not get a simple yes to our litmus test question and they begin a long winded answer refer to rule number one, when someone doesn't know their topic they make it difficult. It is just a ploy to impress upon us how smart they are. But now we are armed with the true meaning of the Constitution and what we have learned is that truly smart people can answer a yes or no question with a "yes" or "no."

In the foregoing pages we saw the Constitution in all of its glorious simplicity. Allow me now to briefly discuss a topic that if not fully resolved will usher in the end of Constitutional rule. Please tell me what is so darn difficult about the following? Article II, Section 1, Clause 5 of the Constitution says, "No person except a natural born Citizen, or a Citizen of the United States, at the time of the Adoption of this Constitution, shall be eligible to the office of President; neither shall any Person be eligible to that Office who shall not have attained to the Age of thirty-five Years, and been fourteen Years a Resident within the United States." In other words to be President of the United States one must meet three requirements (1) be a resident of the US for 14 years, (2) attain the age of 35, (3) be a natural born citizen.

Phillip J. Berg former deputy Attorney General of Pennsylvania on August 21, 2008 filed a suit in Federal Court to determine the Natural Born status of Barack Hussein Obama. At the time of this writing it has yet to be determined. Mr. Berg's suit was dismissed due to lack of standing. In legal parlance to have standing in a law suit one must be sufficiently affected by the matter at hand. Let me get this straight, the possibility that an illegal alien with the help of our Congressmen might be acting as President of the United States does not qualify as something that sufficiently affects every legal citizen in the United States? Perhaps the courts are also complicit. This issue has been in the making during the months of research and writing of this book. It has not been widely reported or written about in the main stream media; perhaps because it is so sensational no one wants to be on the wrong side. Therefore, perhaps everyone is waiting to see how it all shakes out. Political pundits of all stripes are afraid to touch it because fear of being called a 'birther'. Therefore, when a serious even sensational issue like this comes along everyone has elected to take the path of least resistance. However, you can bet the bank on it, when resolved, all the pundits will jump on the wagon and pontificate how they were on the correct side all along. My hope, however, was it would resolve itself prior to publishing. Because, this is a book about the Constitution, if it is ignored and the issue is resolved in the negative after publishing I will be criticized for having ignored the issue. If, on the other hand, it is resolved to the positive one runs the risk of being accused of having been drawn into some wild conspiracy theory. This is not an issue of my making; however, it is of such Constitutional importance it merits mention; If for no other reason the mere discussion of the issue will drive home the importance of living within the framework of the Constitution. The discussion is an object lesson in how something as simple as our Constitution if ignored can cause tremendous consequences for the future.

Regardless of its final outcome allow me to sincerely apologize to you the reader for also dragging you into this. Perhaps one could make the argument that the lack of leadership on both sides of the aisle is forcing us into this discussion. If the issue is positively resolved this entire discussion is for naught. For the sake of the country one can only hope for that disposition. However, God forbid, if it is negatively resolved our leaders in all three branches of government both Republican and Democrats will have severely abdicated their duties and placed this country in a Constitutional crises that has never been contemplated let alone even imagined and it would have been so easy to avoid.

The issue revolves around one man. Although, he is but a single person and if the issue proves to be negatively resolved he alone must bear the burden. However, let us make no mistake about it; he could not have possibly pulled this off without help. More specifically, he would need help from the Democratic National Committee. He would also need help from the leaders of the Democratic Party Nancy Pelosi and Harry Reid. The opposition party is, of course, complicit for not making appropriate challenges in a timely manner. Perhaps calling them the opposition party at this point is giving them credit where none is due. Let us just say if the issue at hand is true the Republican Party is also sullied with very dirty hands. Not a single Congressman will have lived up to their oath of office. I personally emailed my Congressmen and received a barrage of silence.

The magnitude of the offense, if true, will call into question everything our government does from this day forward. Leaders the world over will be unable to trust us. Treaties will be called into question; both, international contracts and our spoken word will fall into distrust. The longer it takes to resolve the greater the peril and the greater the impact for America.

A negative resolution, at this late date, will at the very least cast a pall over our Constitutional form of government and trust at all levels of government. However, Dictators and Tyrants around the world will simply view it as normal operating procedures. Lying and deceit is the normal path to power for them, now they can look at America as if looking into a mirror and see their own reflection.

If positively resolved then we can just write it off as unfortunate fodder that gave rise to an exciting ending to an otherwise mundane topic. Although, it gives me great pause to take something so serious and so dear to my heart as our Constitution and be forced to treat it like a Robert Ludlum spy novel. After so much time has passed even a positive resolution will leave lingering doubts as to why it wasn't presented much sooner. Furthermore, regardless of which side of the issue you may fall, it benefits both sides to have it resolved; an issue so mindlessly simple that only an Ivy League lawyer could possibly have wreaked so much havoc with it.

The simplicity of settling this matter is so profound it defies logic as to why it has not been done. People on both sides are presenting enormously pained arguments; hundreds of thousands of dollars are being spent, thousands of hours wasted for something that everyone in America must at sometime in their life produce. Barack Hussein Obama need only produce his personal records, as every President before him has done, to stop the tremendous divisiveness caused by this issue. After all he did run on a platform of unity, proper documentation would tremendously enhance that position. Make no mistake about it; history will one day expose the truth about the citizenship of Barack Hussein Obama. It is to our benefit to solve the issue now and not wait for the crushing blow of history.

The issue is far greater than the single individual of Barack Hussein Obama. There are millions of registered voters who have a right to know if their candidate is legally qualified.

If the final resolution determines he was not constitutionally qualified, he is not alone in this fraud. Throughout this entire fiasco, not a single elected official has been willing to challenge the issue. During the primary it was the responsibility of the Democratic National Committee and the leaders of the Democratic Party Nancy Pelosi and Harry Reid to vet their candidate for constitutional qualifications. If they have failed their duty or cannot prove to the American voter that due diligence has been performed, then it becomes our right as citizens under the first Amendment guarantee "…to petition the Government for a redress of grievances," to vet our candidates through civil law suits such as the one Mr. Phillip Berg has introduced. To be rebuffed because we do not have standing is a frightening scenario. If we as citizens do not have standing with our own Constitution then who does? When our elected leaders trample the Constitution and we have no recourse to hold them accountable, how does that make our government any different than a dictatorship? This is a slippery slope, from which I hope we can recover. Calling someone names does not solve the issue. Barack Hussein Obama supporters are calling the other side a right wing conspiracy. Why not put a stake in the heart of that conspiracy by simply producing proper documentation?

Some have proffered the argument that a majority of the electorate voted for him so it is a moot issue. If, indeed, that argument proves to be the seminal defense and Barack Hussein Obama is indeed an illegal alien, and allowed to remain in office, the Constitution will effectively no longer be the defining document of the United States. We will be living under mob rule. For if such a ludicrous argument as that stands it brings in yet another Constitutional issue. Article V's entire text is dedicated to the Amendment process. For an illegal alien to become President the Constitution would have to be amended. Nowhere does it say a 51% majority in a Presidential election can amend the Constitution.

As children we were taught not to lie because one lie begets another lie, which begets another lie, and the pattern continues. If Barack Hussein Obama is in fact an illegal alien, allowed to remain in office we are clearly living under a despotic government. For if he is illegal, the minute he took the oath of office to uphold the Constitution he became a liar and fraud. Now, follow me here, one lie begets another lie which begets another lie and so on. The first lie; it is OK to have an illegal alien in the office of President. The second lie, we don't need a Constitutional Amendment the people simply voted. The third lie, no one has standing. If anyone of these is upheld, our Constitution has just been shredded. Therefore, one can see the sheer importance of the issue, by not allowing it to languish in a shroud of controversy. Do you think you would ever get a driver's licenses or passport without documentation? The Presidency carries a far greater importance and one who desires to hide that information brings the cloud of suspicion on himself. Furthermore, when one considers Barack Hussein Obama's past associations with the likes of Jeremiah Wright, his fire and brimstone hate America pastor whose church he attended for twenty years; His close association with domestic terrorist Bill Ayers of whom Obama denied knowing until it was learned he began his political career in Bill Ayers living room; or perhaps his long time relationship with convicted felon Tony Rezko who is serving a prison sentence for fraud. Then there is the issue of the embattled governor of Illinois Rod Blagojevich who Obama categorically denied any association until it was learned his chief of staff Raum Emmanuel was caught on FBI tapes speaking to Blagojevich on several occasions. Now, he blatantly conceals all records that could clear the mystery of his birth and everyone should simply trust him.

When growing up as a child if we strayed ever so slightly to associate with what our parents perceived to be the wrong crowd we were immediately removed from that situation. Why? Our parents and the community clearly understood the ramifications of bad associations. Here we have an individual who hung around with absolutely the worst members of society for all of his formative years then tells us, 'You can trust me, I am not like the others.' That trust he seeks would be tremendously enhanced by proof of citizenship. In the words of George Washington, "Associate with men of good quality if you esteem your own reputation. It is better to be alone than in bad company."

As for me, I am certainly no conspiracy theorists. As stated above it is a constitutional issue that in the context of these pages must be discussed. My lifelong belief in our Republican form of government has held me steadfast to a Constitution that has been equally and fairly applied to all. Furthermore, when a citizen can no longer turn to elected representation or the courts for resolution of such an important event we all have reason to be concerned.

Let us turn to two possible scenarios. First, suppose Barack Hussein Obama is indeed a natural born citizen; then none of the Articles or Amendments of the Constitution mentioned above have been abdicated. The country continues to be governed under the steadfast foundations set forth by our founding fathers and codified by our Constitution. In common parlance we would say, 'no harm, no foul.' Why must the so called educated class take something so simple and make it so difficult? But I digress. To determine this at such a late date, will leave lingering doubt about what took so long. The entire issue could have been put to rest by just producing his birth records, school records and health records as did John McCain when his credentials were called into question. McCain left no doubt, Obama seems to revel in the cloak of mystery he has created, regardless of the possible harm to our country. These are the actions of a selfish individual, not one who places the country first.

In our second scenario Barack Hussein Obama somehow gets through four or eight years of office without a challenge to his citizenship. History, as referenced earlier, will one day expose the truth, as it did with the 40 year 50 billion dollar Ponzi scheme by Bernard Madoff. If he is proven a fraud, everything he did while in office will be called into question; bills, legislation, executive orders, treaties and the longer it takes to discover the greater the peril to our country. Frankly it baffles me as to why, if he is in fact a natural born citizen, would he allow such a cloud to hang over such a great nation. What a great opportunity to disprove millions of nay-Sayers. The single greatest divisive issue created by Barack Hussein Obama could be removed by him. One is reminded of the old saying, 'If it sounds like a duck, looks like a duck and walks like a duck – it is probably a duck.

When a government can create unconstitutional regulations such as the CAFE[47] standards that demonstrably lead to a greater number of deaths, or ban a substance such as DDT, that demonstrably save millions of lives or promulgate a global warming hoax so magnificently as to have the entire world

---

[47] See Appendix: CAFE Standards.

Appendix

The Declaration of Independence

July 4, 1776

When in the Course of human events, it becomes necessary for one people to dissolve the political bands which have connected them with another, and to assume among the powers of the earth, the separate and equal station to which the Laws of Nature and of Nature's God entitle them, a decent respect to the opinions of mankind requires that they should declare the causes which impel them to the separation.

We hold these truths to be self-evident, that all men are created equal, that they are endowed by their Creator with certain unalienable Rights, that among these are Life, Liberty and the pursuit of Happiness. That to secure these rights, Governments are instituted among Men, deriving their just powers from the consent of the governed, That whenever any Form of Government becomes destructive of these ends, it is the Right of the People to alter or to abolish it, and to institute new Government, laying its foundation on such principles and organizing its powers in such form, as to them shall seem most likely to effect their Safety and Happiness. Prudence, indeed, will dictate that Governments long established should not be changed for light and transient causes; and accordingly all experience hath shewn, that mankind are more disposed to suffer, while evils are sufferable, than to right themselves by abolishing the forms to which they are accustomed. But when a long train of abuses and usurpations, pursing invariably the same Object evinces a design to reduce them under absolute Despotism, it is their right, it is their duty, to throw off such Government, and to provide new Guards for their future security. Such has been the patient sufferance of these Colonies; and such is now the necessity which constrains them to alter their former Systems of Government. The history of the present King of Great Britain is a history of repeated injuries and usurpations, all having in direct object the establishment of an absolute Tyranny over these States. To prove this, let Facts be submitted to candid world.

He has refused his Assent to Laws, the most wholesome and necessary for the public good.

He has forbidden his Governors to pass Laws of immediate and pressing importance, unless suspended in their operation till his Assent should be obtained; and when so suspended, he has utterly neglected to attend to them.

He has refused to pass other Laws for the accommodation of large districts of people, unless those people would relinquish the right of Representation in the Legislature, a right inestimable to them and formidable to tyrants only.

He has called together legislative bodies at places unusual, uncomfortable, and distant from the depository of their public Records, for the sole purpose of fatiguing them into compliance with his measures.

He has dissolved Representative Houses repeatedly, for opposing with manly firmness his invasions on the rights of the people.

He has refused for la long time, after such dissolutions, to cause others to be elected; whereby the Legislative powers, incapable of Annihilation, have returned to the People at large for their exercise; the State remaining in the mean time exposed to all the dangers of invasion from without, and convulsions within.

He has endeavoured to prevent the population of these States; for that purpose obstructing the Laws for Naturalization of Foreigners; refusing to pass others to encourage their migrations hither, and raising the conditions of new Appropriations of Lands.

He has obstructed the Administration of Justice, by refusing his Assent to Laws for establishing Judiciary powers.

He has made Judges dependent on his Will along, for the tenure of their offices, and the amount and payment of their salaries.

He has erected a multitude of New Offices, and sent hither swarms of Officers to harass our people, and eat out their substance.

He has kept among us, in times of peace, Standing Armies without the Consent of our legislatures.

He has affected to render the Military independent of and superior to the Civil power.

He has combined with others to subject us to a jurisdiction foreign to our constitution, and unacknowledged by our laws; giving his Assent to their Acts of pretended Legislation:

For Quartering large bodies of armed troops among us:

For protecting them, by a mock Trial, from punishment for any Murders which they should commit on the Inhabitants of these States:

For cutting off our Trade with all parts of the world:

For imposing Taxes on us without our Consent:

For depriving us in many cases, of the benefits of Trial by Jury:

For transporting us beyond Seas to be tried for pretended offences:

For abolishing the free System of English Laws in a neighbouring Province, establishing therein an Arbitrary government, and enlarging its Boundaries so as to render it at once and example and fit instrument for introducing the same absolute rule into these Colonies:

For taking away our Charters, abolishing our most valuable Laws, and altering fundamentally the Forms of our Governments:

For suspending our own Legislatures, and declaring themselves invested with power to legislate for us in all cases whatsoever.

He has abdicated Government here, by declaring us out of his Protection and waging War against us.

He has plundered our seas, ravaged our Coasts, burnt our towns, and destroyed the lives of our people.

He is at this time transporting large Armies of foreign Mercenaries to complete the works of death, desolation and tyranny, already begun with circumstances of Cruelty & perfidy scarcely paralleled in the most barbarous ages, and totally unworthy the Head of a civilized nation.

He has excited domestic insurrections amongst us, and has endeavoured to bring on the inhabitants of our frontiers, the merciless Indian Savages, whose known rule of warfare is an undistinguished destruction of all ages, sexes and conditions.

In every stage of these Oppressions We have Petitioned for Redress in the most humble terms: Our repeated Petitions have been answered only by repeated injury. A prince whose character is thus marked by every act which may define a Tyrant, is unfit to be the ruler of a free people.

Nor have We been wanting in attentions to our British brethren. We have warned them from time to time of attempts by their legislature to extend an unwarrantable jurisdiction over us. We have reminded them of the circumstances of our emigration and settlement here. We have appealed to their native justice and magnanimity, and we have conjured them by the ties of our common kindred to disavow these usurpations, which, would inevitably interrupt our connections and correspondence. They too have been deaf to the voice of justice and of consanguinity. We must, therefore, acquiesce in the necessity, which denounces our Separation, and hold them, as we hold the rest of mankind, Enemies in War, in Peace Friends.

We, therefore, the Representatives of the united States of America, in General Congress, Assembled, appealing to the Supreme Judge of the world for the rectitude of our intentions, do, in the Name, and by Authority of the good People of these Colonies, solemnly publish and declare, That these United Colonies are, and of Right ought to be Free and Independent States; that they are Absolved from all Allegiance to the British Crown, and that all political connection between them and the State of Great Britain, is and ought to be totally dissolved; and that as Free and Independent States, they have full Power to levy War, conclude Peace, contract Alliances, establish Commerce, and to do all other Acts and Things which Independent States may of right do. And for the support of this Declaration, with a firm reliance on the protection of divine Providence, we mutually pledge to each other our Lives, our Fortunes and our sacred Honor.

Georgia:
  Button Gwinnett
  Lyman Hall
  George Walton
North Carolina:
  William Hooper
  Joseph Hewes
  John Penn
South Carolina:
  Edward Rutledge
  Thomas Heyward, Jr.
  Thomas Lynch, Jr.
  Arthur Middleton
Maryland:
  Samuel Chase
  William Paca
  Thomas Stone
  Charles Carroll of Carrollton

Delaware:
  Caesar Rodney
  George Read
  Thomas McKean
New York:
  William Floyd
  Philip Livingston
  Francis Lewis
  Lewis Morris
New Jersey:
  Richard Stockton
  John Witherspoon
  Francis Hopkinson
  John Hart
  Abraham Clark
New Hampshire:
  Josiah Bartlett
  William Whipple
  Matthew Thornton

Virginia:
  George Wythe
  Richard Henry Lee
  Thomas Jefferson
  Benjamin Harrison
  Thomas Nelson, Jr.

Massachusetts:
  John Hancock
  Samuel Adams
  John Adams
  Robert Treat Paine
  Elbridge Gerry

Francis Lightfoot Lee
Carter Braxton

Pennsylvania:
  Robert Morris
  Benjamin Rush
  Benjamin Franklin
  John Morton
  George Clymer
  James Smith
  George Taylor
  James Wilson
  George Ross

Rhode Island:
  Stephen Hopkins
  William Ellery

Connecticut:
  Roger Sherman
  Samuel Huntington
  William Williams
  Oliver Wolcott

THE CONSTITUTION OF THE UNITED STATES OF AMERICA

We the People of the United States, in Order to form a more perfect Union, establish Justice, insure domestic Tranquility, provide for the common defence, promote the general Welfare, and secure the Blessings of Liberty to ourselves and our Posterity, do ordain and establish this Constitution for the United States of America.

Article I

Section. 1. All legislative Powers herein granted shall be vested in a Congress of the United States, which shall consist of a Senate and House of Representatives.

Section. 2. The House of Representatives shall be composed of Members chosen every second Year by the People of the several States, and the Electors in each State shall have the Qualifications requisite for Electors of the most numerous Branch of the State Legislature.

No person shall be a Representative who shall not have attained to the Age of twenty five Years, and been seven Years a Citizen of the United States, and who shall not, when elected, be an Inhabitant of that State in which he shall be chosen.

(Representatives and direct Taxes shall be apportioned among the several States which may be included within this Union, according to their respective Numbers, which shall be determined by adding to the whole Number of free Persons, including those bound to Service for a Term of Years, and excluding Indians not taxed, three fifths of all other Persons.)[48] The actual Enumeration shall be made within three Years after the first Meeting of the Congress of the United States, and

---

[48] Changed by Section 2 of the Fourteenth Amendment

within every subsequent Term of ten Years, in such Manner as they shall by Law direct. The Number of Representatives shall not exceed one for every thirty Thousand, but each State shall have at Least one Representative; and until such enumeration shall be made, the State of New Hampshire shall be entitled to chuse three, Massachusetts eight, Rhode-Island and Providence Plantations one, Connecticut five, New-York six, New Jersey four, Pennsylvania eight, Delaware one, Maryland six, Virginia ten, North Carolina five, South Carolina five and Georgia three.

When vacancies happen in the Representation from any State, the Executive Authority thereof shall issue Writs of Election to fill such Vacancies.

The House of Representatives shall chuse their Speaker and other Officers; and shall have the sole Power of Impeachment.

Section. 3. The Senate of the United States shall be composed of two Senators from each State, (chosen by the Legislature thereof,)[49] for six Years; and each Senator shall have one Vote.

Immediately after they shall be assembled in Consequence of the first Election, they shall be divided as equally as many be into three Classes. The Seats of the Senators of the first Class shall be vacated at the Expiration of the second Year, of the second Class at the Expiration of the fourth Year, and of the third Class at the Expiration of the sixth Year, so that one third may be chosen every second Year; (and if Vacancies happen by Resignation, or otherwise, during the Recess of the Legislature of any State, the Executive thereof may make temporary

---

[49] Changed by the Seventeenth Amendment

Appointment until the next Meeting of the Legislature, which shall then fill such Vacancies.)[50]

No person shall be a Senator who shall not have attained to the Age of thirty Years, and been nine Years a Citizen of the United States, and who shall not, when elected, be an Inhabitatnt of that State for which he shall be chosen.

The Vice President of the United States shall be President of the Senate, but shall have no Vote, unless they be equally divided.

The Senate shall chuse their other Officers, and also a President pro tempore, in the Absence of the Vice President, or when he shall exercise the Office of President of the United States.

The Senate shall have the sole Power to try all Impeachments. When sitting for that Purpose, they shall be on Oath or Affirmation. When the President of the United States is tried, the Chief Justice shall preside: And no Person shall be convicted without the Concurrence of two thirds of the Members present.

Judgment in Cases of Impeachment shall not extend further than to removal from Office, and disqualification to hold and enjoy any Office of honor, Trust or Profit under the United States: but the Party convicted shall nevertheless be liable and subject to Indictment, Trial, Judgment and Punishment, according to Law.

Section. 4. The Times, Places and Manner of holding Elections for Senators and Representatives, shall be prescribed in each State by the Legislature thereof; but the Congress may at any time by Law make or alter such Regulations, except as to the Places of chusing Senators.

---

[50] Changed by the Seventeenth Amendment

The Congress shall assemble at least once in every Year, and such Meeting shall be (on the first Monday in December,)[51] unless they shall by Law appoint a different Day.

Section. 5. Each House shall b e the Judge of the Elections, Returns and Qualifications of its own Members, and a Majority of each shall constitute a Quorum to do Business; but a smaller number may adjourn from day to day, and may be authorized to compel the Attendance of absent Members, in such Manner, and under such Penalties as each House may provide.

Each House may determine the Rules of its Proceedings, punish its Members for disorderly Behaviour, and, with the Concurrence of two thirds, expel a Member.

Each House shall keep a Journal of its Proceedings, and from time to time publish the same, excepting such Parts as may in their Judgment require Secrecy; and the Yeas and Nays of the Members of either House on any question shall, at the Desire of one fifth of those Present, be entered on the Journal.

Neither House, during the Session of Congress, shall, without the Consent of the other, adjourn for more than three days, nor to any other Place than that in which the two Houses shall be sitting.

Section. 6. The Senators and Representatives shall receive a Compensation for their Services, to be ascertained by Law, and paid out of the Treasury of the United States. They shall in all Cases, except Treason, Felony and Breach of the Peace, be privileged from Arrest during their Attendance at the Session of their respective Houses, and in going to and returning from the same; and for any Speech or Debate in either House, they shall not be questioned in any other Place.

---

[51] Changed by Section 2 of the Twentieth Amendment

No Senator or Representative shall, during the Time for which he was elected, be appointed to any civil Office under the Authority of the United States, which shall have been created, or the Emoluments whereof shall have been increased during such time; and no Person holding any Office under the United States, shall be a Member of either House during his Continuance in Office.

Section. 7. All bills for raising Revenue shall originate in the House of Representatives; but the Senate may propose or concur with Amendments as on other Bills.

Every Bill which shall have passed the House of Representatives and the Senate, shall, before it become a Law, be presented to the President of the United States: If he approve he shall sign it, but if not he shall return it, with his Objections to that House in which it shall have originated, who shall enter the Objections at large on their Journal, and proceed to reconsider it. If after such Reconsideration two thirds of that of that House shall agreed to pass the Bill, it shall be sent, together with the Objections, to the other House, by which it shall likewise be reconsidered, and if approved by two thirds of that House, it shall become a Law. But in all such Cases the Votes of both Houses shall be determined by yeas and Nays, and the Names of the Persons voting for and against the Bill shall be entered on the Journal of each House respectively. If any Bill shall not be returned by the President within ten Days (Sundays excepted) after it shall have been presented to him, the Same shall be a Law, in like Manner as if he had signed it, unless the Congress by their Adjournment prevent its Return, in which Case it shall not be a Law.

Every Order, Resolution, or Vote to which the Concurrence of the Senate and House of Representatives may be necessary (except on a question of Adjournment) shall be presented to the President of the United States; and before the Same shall take Effect, shall be approved by him, or being disapproved by him, shall be repassed by two thirds of the Senate and House of Representatives, according to the Rules and Limitations prescribed in the Case of a Bill.

Section. 8. The Congress shall have Power To lay and collect Taxes, Duties, Imposts and Excises, to pay the Debts and provide for the common Defence and general Welfare of the United States; but all Duties, Imposts and Excises shall be uniform throughout the United States;

To borrow money on the credit of the United States;

To regulate Commerce with foreign Nations, and among the several States, and with the Indian Tribes;

To establish an uniform Rule of Naturalization, and uniform Laws on the subject of Bankruptcies throughout the United States;

To coin Money, regulate the Value thereof, and of foreign Coin, and fix the Standard of Weights and Measures;

To provide for the Punishment of counterfeiting the Securities and current Coin of the United States;

To establish Post Offices and post Roads;

To promote the Progress of Science and useful Arts, by securing for limited Times to Authors and Inventors the exclusive Right to their respective Writings and Discoveries;

To constitute Tribunal inferior to the supreme Court;

To define and punish Piracies and Felonies committed on the high Seas, and Offenses against the Law of Nations;

To declare War, grant Letters of Marque and Reprisal, and make Rules concerning Captures on Land and Water;

To raise and support Armies, but no Appropriation of Money to that Use shall be for a longer Term than two Years;

To provide and maintain a Navy;

To make Rules for the Government and Regulation of the land and naval Forces;

To provide for calling forth the Militia to execute the Laws of the Union, suppress Insurrections and repel Invasions;

To provide for organizing, arming, and disciplining, the Militia, and for governing such Part of them as may be employed in the Service of the United States, reserving to the States respectively, the Appointment of the officers, and the Authority of training the Militia according to the discipline prescribed by Congress;

To exercise exclusive Legislation in all Cases whatsoever, over such District (not exceeding ten Miles square) as may, by Cession of particular States, and the Acceptance of Congress, become the Seat of the Government of the United States, and to exercise like Authority over all Places purchased by the Consent of the Legislature of the State in which the Same shall be, for the Erection of Forts, Magazines, Arsenals, dockyards, and other needful Buildings; - And

To make all Laws which shall be necessary and proper for carrying into Execution the foregoing Powers, and all other Powers vested by this Constitution in the Government of the United States, or in any Department or Officer thereof.

Section. 9. The Migration of Importation of such Persons as any of the States now existing shall think proper to admit, shall not be prohibited by the Congress prior to the Year one thousand eight hundred and eight, but a Tax on or duty may be imposed on such Importation, not exceeding ten dollars for each Person.

The Privilege of the Writ of Habeas Corpus shall not be suspended, unless when in Cases of Rebellion or Invasion the public Safety may require it.

No Bill of Attainder or ex post facto Law shall be passed.

No Capitation, or other direct, Tax shall be laid, unless in Proportion to the Census or Enumeration herein before directed to be taken.[52]

No Tax or Duty shall be laid on Articles exported from any State.

No Preference shall be given by any Regulation of Commerce or Revenue to the Ports of one State over those of another; nor shall Vessels bound to, or from, one State, be obliged to enter, clear, or pay Duties in another.

No Money shall be drawn from the Treasury, but in Consequence of Appropriations made by Law; and a regular Statement and Account of the Receipts and Expenditures of all public Money shall be published from time to time.

No Title of Nobility shall be granted by the United States: And no person holding any Office of Profit or Trust under them, shall, without the Consent of the Congress, accept of any present, Emolument, Office, or Title, of any kind whatever, from any King, Prince or foreign State.

Section. 10. No State shall enter into any Treaty, Alliance, or Confederation; grant Letters of Marque and Reprisal; coin Money; emit Bills of Credit; make any Thing but gold and silver Coin a Tender in Payment of Debts; pass any Bill of Attainder, ex post facto Law, or Law impairing the Obligation of Contracts, or grant any Title of Nobility.

---

[52] See Sixteenth Amendment

No State shall, without the Consent of the Congress, lay any Imposts or Duties on Imports or Exports, except what may be absolutely necessary for executing it's inspection Laws: and the net Produce of all Duties and posts, laid by any State on Imports or Exports, shall be for the Use of the Treasury of the United States; and all such Laws shall be subject to the Revision and Controul of the Congress.

No State shall, without the Consent of Congress lay any duty of Tonnage, keep Troops, or Ships of War in time of Peace, enter into any Agreement or Compact with another State,. Or with a foreign Power, or engage in War, unle4ss actually invaded, or in such imminent Danger as will not admit of delay.

Article II

Section. 1. The executive Power shall be vested in a President of the United States of America. He shall hold his Office during the Term of four Years, and, together with the Vice-President chosen for the same Term, be elected, as follows:

Each State shall appoint, in such Manner as the Legislature thereof may direct, a Number of Electors, equal to the whole Number of Senators and Representatives to which the State may be entitled in the Congress: but no Senator or Representative, or Person holding an Office of Trust or Profit under the United States, shall be appointed an Elector.

(The Electors shall meet in their respective States, and vote by Ballot for two Persons, of whom on at least shall not be an Inhabitant of the same State with themselves. And they shall make a List of all the Persons voted for, and of the Number of Votes for each; which List they shall sign and certify, and transmit sealed to the Seat of the Government of the United

States, directed to the President of the Senate. The President of the Senate shall, in the Presence of the Senate and House of Representatives, open all the Certificates, and the Votes shall then be counted. The Person having thre greatest Number of Votes shall be the president, if such Number be a Majority of the whole Number of Electors appointed; and if there be more than one who have such Majority, and have an equal Number o Votes, then the House of Representatives shall immediately chuse by Ballot one of them for President; and if no Person have a Majority, then from the five highest on the List the said House shall in like Manner chuse the President. But in chusing the President, the Votes shall be taken by States, the Representation from each State having one Vote; a quorum for this Purpose shall consist of a Member or Members from two-thirds of the States, and a Majority of all the States shall be necessary to a Choice. In every Case, after the Choice of the President, the Person having the greatest Number of Votes of the Electors shall be the Vice President. But if there should remain two or more who have equal Votes, the Senate shall chuse from them by Ballot the Vice President.)[53]

The Congress may determine the Time of chusing the Electors, and the Day on which they shall give their Votes; which Day shall be the same throughout the United States.

No person except a natural born Citizen, or a Citizen of the United States, at the time of the Adoption of this Constitution, shall be eligible to the Office of President; neither shall any Person be eligible to that Office who shall not have attained to the Age of thirty-five Years, and been fourteen years a Resident within the United States.

---

[53] Changed by the Twelfth Amendment

(In Case of the Removal of the President from Office, or of his Death, Resignation, or Inability to discharge the Powers and Duties of the said Office, the Same shall devolve on the Vic President, and the Congress may by Law provide for the Case of Removal, Death, Resignation or Inability, both of the President and Vice President, declaring what Officer shall then act as President, and such Officer shall act accordingly, until the Disability be removed, or a President shall be elected.)[54]

The President shall, at stated Times, receive for his Services, a Compensation, which shall neither be increased nor diminished during the Period for which he shall have been elected, and he shall not receive within that Period any other Emolument from the United States, or any of them.

Before he enter on the Execution of his Office he shall take the following Oath or Affirmation: - "I do solemnly swear (or affirm) that I will faithfully execute the Office of President of the United States, and will to the best of my Ability, preserve, protect and defend the Constitution of the United States."

Section. 2. The President shall be Commander in Chief of the Army and Navy of the United States, and of the Militia of the several States, when called into the actual Service of the United States; he may require the Opinion, in writing, of the principal Officer in each of the executive Departments, upon any subject relating to the Duties of their respective Offices, and he shall have Power to grant Reprieves and Pardons for offenses against the United States, except in Cases of Impeachment.

He shall have Power, by and with the Advice and Consent of the Senate, to make Treaties, provided two thirds of the Senators present concur; and he shall nominate, and by and with the Advice and Consent of the Senate, shall appoint

---

[54] Changed by the Twenty-Fifth Amendment

Ambassadors, other public Ministers and Consuls, Judges of the supreme Court, and all other Officers of the United States, whose Appointments are not herein otherwise provided for, and which shall be established by Law: but the Congress may by Law vest the Appointment of such inferior Officers, as they think proper, in the President alone, in the Courts of Law, or in the Heads of Departments.

The President shall have Power to fill up all Vacancies that may happen during the Recess of the Senate, by granting Commissions which shall expire at the End of their next Session.

Section. 3. He shall from time to time give to the Congress Information of the State of the Union, and recommend to their Consideration such Measures as he shall judge necessary and expedient; he may, on extraordinary Occasions, convene both Houses, or either of them, and in Case of Disagreement between them, with Respect to the Time of Adjournment, he may adjourn them to such Time as he shall think proper; he shall receive Ambassadors and other public Ministers; he shall take Care that the Laws be faithfully executed, and shall Commission all the Officers of the United States.

Section. 4. The President, Vice President and all civil Officers of the United States, shall be removed from Office on Impeachment for, and Conviction of, Treason, Bribery, or other high Crimes and Misdemeanors.

Article III

Section. 1. The judicial Power of the United States, shall be vested in one supreme Court, and in such inferior Courts as the Congress may from time to time ordain and establish. The Judges, both of the supreme and inferior Courts, shall hold their Offices during good Behaviour, and shall, at stated Times receive for their Services a Compensation which shall not be diminished during their Continuance in Office.

Section. 2. The judicial Power shall extend to all Cases, in Law and Equity, arising under this Constitution, the Laws of the United States, and Treaties made, or which shall be made, under their Authority;-to all Cases affecting Ambassadors, other public Ministers and Consuls;-to all Cases of admiralty and maritime Jurisdiction; to Controversies to which the United States shall be a Party;-to Controversies between two or more States;-(between a State and Citizens of another State;-)[55] between Citizens of different States;-between Citizens of the same State claiming Lands under Grants of different States, (and between a State, or the Citizens thereof, and foreign States, Citizens or Subjects.)[56]

In all Cases affecting Ambassadors, other public Ministers and Consuls, and those in which a State shall be Party, the supreme Court shall have original Jurisdiction. In all the other Cases before mentioned, the supreme Court shall have appellate Jurisdiction, both as to Law and Fact, with such Exceptions, and under such Regulations as the Congress shall make.

The Trial of all Crimes, except in Cases of Impeachment, shall be by Jury; and such Trial shall be held in the State where the said Crimes shall have been committed; but when not committed within any State, the Trial shall be at such Place or Places as the Congress may by Law have directed.

---

[55] Changed by the Eleventh Amendment
[56] Changed by the Eleventh Amendment

Article VI

All Debts contracted and Engagements entered into, before the Adoption of this Constitution, shall be as valid against the United States under this Constitution, as under the Confederation.

This Constitution, and the Laws of the United States which shall be made in Pursuance thereof; and all Treaties made, or which shall be made, under the Authority of the United States, shall be the supreme Law of the Land; and the Judges in every State shall be bound thereby, any Thing in the Constitution or Laws of any State to the Contrary notwithstanding.

The Senators and Representatives before mentioned, and the Members of the several State Legislatures, and all executive and judicial Officers, both of the United States and of the several States, shall be bound by Oath or Affirmation, to support this Constitution; but no religious Test shall ever be required as a Qualification to any Office or public Trust under the United States.

Article VII

The Ratification of the Conventions of nine States shall be sufficient for the Establishment of this Constitution between the States so ratifying the Same.

Done in Convention by the Unanimous Consent of the States present the Seventeenth Day of September in the Year of our lord one thousand seven hundred and Eighty seven and of the Independence of the Unites States of America the Twelfth in Witness whereof We have hereunto subscribed our Names.

G. Washington
President and deputy from Virginia

Delaware	Geo: Read
	Gunning Bedford jun
	John Dickinson
	Richard Bassett
	Jaco: Broom
Maryland	James McHenry
	Dan of St Thos. Jenifer
	Danl. Carroll
Virginia	John Blair
	James Madison Jr.
North Carolina	Wm. Blount
	Richd. Dobbs Spaight
	Hu Williamson
South Carolina	J. Rutledge
	Charles Cotesworth Pinckney
	Charles Pinckney
Georgia	William Few
	Abr Baldwin
New Hampshire	John Langdon
	Nicholas Gilman
Massachusetts	Nathaniel Gorham
	Rufus King

Connecticut	Wm. Saml. Johnson
	Roger Sherman
New York	Alexander Hamilton
New Jersey	Wil: Livingston
	David Brealey
	Wm. Paterson
	Jona: Dayton
Pensylvania[58]	B Franklin
	Thomas Mifflin
	Robt. Morris
	Geo. Clymer
	Thos. FitzSimons
	Jared Ingersoll
	James Wilson
	Gouv Morris
	Attest William Jackson Secretary

---

[58] This incorrect spelling of Pennsylvania was in the original document

THE FIXED HISTORY OF 435 REPRESENTATIVES:

There is nothing magical about the number of Representatives being set at 435. It is, however, more a function of an arrogant Congress than anything else. Keep in mind the purpose of this book is to explain the Constitution in terms that we can all understand; by so doing we gain a clear insight into the soul of a corrupt Congress.

The number 435, was not selected by the founders, it was never ratified by the 50 states. It was simply the creation of another corrupt Congress who had little regard for the Constitution. After President George Washington vetoed the first apportionment bill in April 1792, the House of Representatives voted to change the representation ratio to thirty-three thousand instead of the constitutionally mandated thirty-thousand. That is it, they just took a vote and this method of assigning representation by congressional act became kwon as the 'fixed ratio' method. Congress used this method until the 1920 census.

In 1920 for the first time in our history, after the census showed an increase in population, no new House members were added. This situation remained static for some nine years when in 1929, just before the great depression, the 70th Congress passed a law known as 2U.S.C. Sec. 2, Election of Senators and Representatives, fixing the House of Representatives at 435. The law is unconstitutional for at least two reasons: one, it contravenes the numbers stated in Article I, Section 2, Clause 3. Two, it completely ignores Article V procedures for amending the Constitution.

With that said let us not get too worked up about a corrupt congress quite yet. Although, the method by which Congress chose to fix the number at 435 was an in-your-face move around the Constitution there is sufficient evidence by our founding fathers whereby they fully expected the House to one day be a fixed number. Consider Federalists 55 where James Madison is clearly grappling with the issue of the proper number of members for the House of Representatives, when he says, "... no political problem is less susceptible of a precise solution than that which relates to the number most convenient for a representative legislature..." The Country and its Constitution was still in its infancy and Madison did not want to pre-maturely assign a fixed number at such an early date. However, he did recognize a fixed number to be beneficial; he only thought it would come by way of the amendment process. Madison continues, "Sixty or Seventy men may be more properly trusted with a given degree of power than six or seven. But it does not follow that six or seven hundred would be proportionably a better depositary. And if we carry on the supposition to six or seven thousand, the whole reasoning ought to be reversed. The truth is, that in all cases a certain number at least seems to be necessary to secure the benefits of free consultation and discussion, and to guard against too easy a combination for improper purposes; as, on the other hand, the number ought at most to be kept within a certain limit, in order to avoid the confusion and intemperance of a multitude." The fixed number of Representatives at 435 seems to have served us well; one just gets an uneasy feeling when Congress can at will change the Constitution.

THE JUDICIARY

In Federalists 37 Madison said, "The ultimate object of these papers is to determine clearly and fully the merits of this Constitution." Hamilton in Federalists 78 expected the powers of the judiciary to be minimal when he says, "The judiciary... will always be the least dangerous to the political rights of the Constitution." For Hamilton, "The rules of legal interpretation are rules of common sense." (Federalists 83) **NEVER** was the Judiciary intended to legislate from the bench or overturn the will of the people as we too often see today.

Consistent with the founding fathers, Michigan Supreme Court Justice Stephen Markman had this to say, "The highest example of judicial duty is to subordinate one's personal will and one's private views to the law. The responsible judge must subordinate his personal sense of justice to the public justice of our Constitution and its representative and legal institutions. The founding fathers never envisioned an activists Judiciary. It is simply the duty of the judge to say what the law "is" and not what it "ought" to be."

There are numerous examples but we will only look at two. The first one, in November 1996 the California voters passed a state constitutional amendment   known as prop 209 which outlawed discrimination and preferential treatment. District court Judge Thelton Henderson blocked enforcement of the amendment. This is exactly the kind of action by a judiciary Madison and Hamilton would be opposed to. A Judge is not to make law that is the responsibility of the legislature who are elected by the people. A judge should never be making law; his job is only to interpret it. Note: A three judge panel in the U.S. Ninth Circuit Court of appeals subsequently overturned that ruling. However, our next example is a much more egregious one of Judges legislating from the bench. A decision that to this day stands, but is clearly unconstitutional.

On January 22, 1973 The Nation's highest court affirmed abortion as a national right guaranteed by the Constitution. This is wrong on so many levels but we will only address a few of them here. First it is not the intent of this book to argue for or against Roe v. Wade, it is merely to demonstrate how even the Supreme Court of the land has no jurisdiction to legislate from the bench. There is not a single paragraph, sentence, or word in the Constitution that could lead anyone to such a convoluted decision. Walter E. Williams said, "Some ideas are so crazy that only a politician could believe them." My reference here is the term used to arrive at the court's decision was based on 'penumbras.' By definition a penumbra is nothing more than an implication. As we have learned throughout this book the Constitution was written in common everyday language of the day. It is not a legal guideline subject to interpretation by lawyers; it is the supreme law of the land not written in legalese but in the language common to the day so that all could "clearly" understand their rights. Any time a decision is based on a so called 'penumbra' it is doubtful at best. If we learn one thing from this book it should be this: *when in doubt, the states win out.* This is not a decision as Hamilton said of common sense; the decision of abortion belongs to the purview of the Sovereign States.

The will of the people under our Constitution is expressed through an elected legislature, not the unelected Judiciary. When the Constitution is silent on an issue the will of the people becomes the individual will of the Sovereign States. More often than not, today the will of the people is usurped by a vocal and liberal minority who cannot win in the arena of ideas but must work through a corrupted liberal Judge who is willing to legislate from the bench. The actions of these judges are not those characterized by Hamilton as "the least dangerous."

THOMAS JEFFERSON

The entire argument today for removing all references of religion from the public square is based on the well known quote from Thomas Jefferson when he wrote in a letter to the Danbury Baptist Association in 1802 there was a, "Wall of separation between church and state." This is such a specious argument as to make it laughable. First, note the date was 1802, more than ten years after the ratification of the Bill of Rights. Next, Thomas Jefferson had absolutely no role in drafting the well known Establishment Clause. Furthermore, he was neither a member of the first Congress that drafted the First Amendment and sent it to the states for ratification nor was he a member of the Virginia General Assembly that voted to ratify it.

This book is about understanding the Constitution and the intentions of our founding fathers. Therefore, we must look to James Madison, the father of the Constitution and author of Bill of Rights and the first Amendment. During the ratification of the Bill of Rights a Connecticut Congressman expressed concern that this Amendment would interfere with his state's established church and religious policy, to which Madison answered, "...that it would not." In 1785 he also said, "We have staked the whole future of American civilization, not upon the power of government, far from it. We have staked the future of all of our political institutions...upon the capacity of each and all of us to govern ourselves, to sustain ourselves according to the Ten Commandments of God." Madison also had the following to say regards religion, "belief in a God All Powerful wise and good, is so essential to the moral order of the World and to the happiness of man, that arguments which enforce it cannot be drawn from too many sources."

THE DRAFT

It has been argued that the military draft is unconstitutional; it is not. In the Selective Draft Law Case of 1918 Chief Justice Roger B. Taney wrote for the majority when he said selective service was constitutional. The decision, although correct, is fatally flawed in its reasoning. It was largely based on citing the contemporary practices in the German Empire, Austrian Empire, Russian Empire, Turkish Empire, British Empire, Japanese Empire...etc. We should never look to foreign powers to interpret our Constitution.

The central theme of this book is what did the founding fathers intend? This is an easy one, the aforementioned decision need only look at Hamilton and Federalists 23 where in one part he says in reference to raising armies, "...that there can be no limitation of that authority which is to provide for the defense and protection of the community in any manner essential to its efficacy. " One means of efficacy is certainly the draft. Further along in Federalists 23 Hamilton says, "The authorities essential to the common defense are these: to raise armies; to build and equip fleets; to prescribe rules for the government of both; to direct their operations; to provide for their support. These powers ought to exist without limitation." To call the draft unconstitutional would certainly place limitations on this plenary power.

CAFE STANDARDS

Corporate Average Fuel Economy standards were enacted by our congressmen in 1975. The single stated purpose of this regulation was to reduce energy consumption by increasing the fuel economy of automobiles; just another attempt of the know-it-all legal profession to save the world. Since its inception our congressmen have continued to increase the standards to such a point that the only way for an auto maker to remain compliant was to down size their fleets, by making smaller and lighter automobiles, causing the death of many which continues to this day.

Consider the following study by the National Center for Public Policy Research:

According to a 2003 NHTSA study, when a vehicle is reduced by 100 pounds the estimated fatality rate increases as much as 5.63 percent for light automobiles weighing less than 2,950 pounds, 4.7 percent for heavier automobiles weighing over 2,950 pounds and 3.06 percent for light trucks. Between model years 1996 and 1999, these rates translated into additional traffic fatalities of 13,608 for light automobiles, 10,884 for heavier automobiles and 14,705 for light trucks.

A 2001 National Academy of Sciences panel found that constraining automobile manufactures to produce smaller, lighter vehicles in the 1970s and early 1980s probably resulted in an additional 1,300 to 2,600 traffic fatalities in 1993 alone.

An extensive 1999 USA Today analysis of crash data found that since CAFE went into effect in 1978, 46,000 people died in crashes they otherwise would have survived, had they been in bigger, heavier vehicles. This, according to a 1999 USA Today analysis of crash data since 1975, roughly figures to be

7,700 deaths for every mile per gallon gained in fuel economy standards.

The USA Today report also said smaller automobiles – such as the Chevrolet Cavalier or Dodge Neon – accounted for 12,144 fatalities or 37 percent of vehicle deaths in 1997, though such automobiles comprised only 18 percent of all vehicles.

A 1989 Harvard-Brookings study estimated CAFE to be responsible for 2,200-3,900 excess occupant fatalities over ten years of a given automobiles model years use. Moreover, the researchers estimated between 11,000 and 19,500 occupants would suffer serious but nonfatal crash injuries as a result of CAFE.

The same Harvard-Brookings study found CAFE had resulted in a 500-pound weight reduction of the average automobile. As a result, occupants were put at a 14 to 27 percent greater risk of traffic death.

Passengers in small automobiles die at a much higher rate when involved in traffic accidents with large automobiles. Traffic safety expert Dr. Leonard Evans estimates that drivers in lighter automobiles may be 12 times as likely to be killed in a crash when the other vehicle is twice as heavy as the lighter automobile.

All this brought to us by our congressmen who say only they can run an efficient health care system, and only they with their all knowing intellect can save the world from global warming. If you want more death and destruction, simply continue to vote for that wonderful Congressman who seems so nice.

QUOTABLE QUOTES FROM OUR FOUNDING FATHERS

"...we mutually pledge to each other our Lives, our Fortunes and our sacred Honor."
Thomas Jefferson, Declaration of Independence

"Of all the dispositions and habits which lead to political prosperity, religion and morality are indispensable supports."
"...reason and experience both forbid us to expect that national morality can prevail in exclusion of religious principle."
George Washington, Farewell Address September, 17 1796

"Since the general civilization of mankind I believe there are more instances of the abridgment of the freedom of the people by gradual and silent encroachments of those in power than by violent and sudden usurpations."
James Madison, June 6, 1788

"Firearms stand next in importance to the Constitution itself. They are the American people's liberty, teeth and keystone under independence. The church, the plow, the prairie wagon, and citizen's firearms are indelibly related. From the hour the Pilgrims landed, to the present day, events, occurrences, and tendencies prove that to insure peace, security, and happiness, the rifle and pistol are equally indispensable. Every corner of this land owns firearms, and more than 99-99/100percent of them by their silence indicate they are in safe and sane hand s. The atmosphere of firearms anywhere and everywhere restrains evil interference – they deserve a place of honor with all that's good. When firearms go, all goes – we need them every hour."
George Washington, address to Congress

"...arms...discourage and keep the plunderer in awe, and preserve order in the world as well as property...Horrid mischief would ensue were the law-abiding deprived of the use of them."
Thomas Paine, 1775

"Laws that forbid the carrying of arms...disarm only those who are neither inclined nor determined to commit crimes...Such laws make things worse for the assaulted and better for the assailants; they serve rather to encourage than to prevent homicides, for an unarmed man may be attacked with greater confidence than an armed man."
Thomas Jefferson, 1764

"Resistance to tyranny is obedience to God"
Thomas Jefferson

"Guard with jealous attention the public liberty. Suspect everyone who approaches that jewel. Unfortunately, nothing will preserve it but downright force. Whenever you give up that force you are ruined...The great object is that every man be armed...Everyone who is able may have a gun."
Patrick Henry

"A strong body makes the mind strong. As to the species of exercises, I advise the gun. While this gives a moderate exercise to the Body, it gives boldness, enterprise and independence to the mind. Games played with the ball, and others of that nature, are too violent for the body and stamp no character on the mind. Let you gun therefore be the constant companion of your walks."
Thomas Jefferson

"Americans have the advantage of being armed-unlike the citizens of other countries where the governments are afraid to trust the people with arms."
James Madison

"God grants liberty only to those who love it and are always ready to guard and defend it."
Daniel Webster

"Constitution shall never be construed...to prevent the people of the United States who are peaceable citizens from keeping their own arms."
Samuel Adams

"The best we can hope for concerning the people at large is that they be properly armed."
Alexander Hamilton
"To disarm the people is the best and most effectual way to enslave them."
George Mason

"I would rather be exposed to the inconveniences attending too much liberty than to those attending too small a degree of it."
Thomas Jefferson

"He who dares not offend cannot be honest."
Thomas Paine

"Congress has not unlimited powers to provide for the general welfare but only those specifically enumerated."
Thomas Jefferson

"The powers of the federal government are enumerated; it can only operate in certain cases; it has legislative powers on defined and limited objects, beyond which it cannot extend its jurisdiction."
James Madison, June 6, 1788

"I only regret that I have but one life to lose for my country."
Nathan Hale, September 22, 1776

"When the people find that they can vote themselves money that will herald the end of the republic."
Benjamin Franklin

"The government of the United States is a definite government, confined to specified objects. It is not like the state governments, whose powers are more general. Charity is no part of the legislative duty of the government."
James Madison.
"No nation was ever ruined by trade, even seemingly the most disadvantageous."
Benjamin Franklin, 1774

"Were we directed from Washington when to sow, and when to reap, we should soon want bread."
Thomas Jefferson, Autobiography 1821"

"Those who expect to reap the blessings of freedom, must, like men, undergo the fatigues of supporting it."
Thomas Paine, September 11, 1777

"The moment the idea is admitted into society that property is not as sacred as the laws of God, and that there is not a force of law and public justice to protect it, anarchy and tyranny commence. If 'Thou shalt not covet' and 'Thou shalt not steal' were not commandments of Heaven, they must be made inviolable precepts in every society before it can be civilized or made free."
John Adams 1787

"To be prepared for war, is one of the most effectual means of preserving peace."
George Washington, January 8, 1790

"The legitimate powers of government extend to such acts only as are injurious to others. But it does me no injury for my neighbor to say there are twenty gods, or no God. It neither picks my pocket nor breaks my leg."
Thomas Jefferson

"One single object...will merit the endless gratitude of the society: that of restraining the judges from usurping legislation."
Thomas Jefferson, March 25, 1825

"Remember democracy never lasts long. It soon wastes, exhausts, and murders itself. There never was a democracy yet that did not commit suicide."
John Adams, April 15, 1814

"To take from one, because it is thought his own industry and that of his fathers has acquired too much, in order to spare

to others, who, or whose fathers, have not exercised equal industry and skill, is to violate arbitrarily the first principle of association, the guarantee to everyone the free exercise of his industry and the fruits acquired by it."
Thomas Jefferson, April 6, 1816

"I am for doing good to the poor, but I differ in opinion of the means. I think the best way of doing good to the poor, is not making them easy in poverty, bet leading or driving them out of it."
Benjamin Franklin

"The purpose of a written constitution is to bind up the several branches of government by certain laws, which, when they transgress, their acts shall become nullities; to render unnecessary an appeal to the people, or in other words a rebellion, on every infraction of their rights, on the peril that their acquiescence shall be construed into an intention to surrender those rights."
Thomas Jefferson, 1782

"It is not the function of our Government to keep the citizen from falling into error; it is the function of the citizen to keep the government from falling into error."
Justice Robert Jackson, 1892-1954

"...a state must resist federal enforcement of an unconstitutional and dangerous policy."
Thomas Jefferson and James Madison

BIBLIOGRAPHY

Hamilton, Alexander; Jay, John; Madison, James; *The Federalists Papers* (1787-1788).

Corace, Don, *Government Pirates The Assault on Private Property Rights.* Haper Collings (2008).

Gutzman, Kevin R.C., *The Politically Incorrect Guide to the Constitution.* Regnery Publishing (2007).

Gross, Martin L., *The Political Racket.* Random House (1996) Ballantine Books.

Henry, H. Lon, Congress: *Americas Privileged Class.* Prima Publishing (1994).

Levin, Mark, *Men In Black.* Regnery Publishing (2005).

Napolitano, Judge Andrew P., *The Constitution in Exile.* Nelson Current Books (2006).

Robertson, Pat., *Courting Disaster.* Integrity Publishers (2004).

Sandefur, Timothy, *Property Rights n 21ˢᵗ Century America.* Cato Institute (2006).

Williams, Walter E., *Liberty Versus The Tyranny of Socialism.* Hoover Inst. Pr; 1ˢᵗ edition (2008)

Williams, Walter E., *More Liberty Means Less Government.* Hoover Institution Press (1999). Stanford University.

Woods, Thomas E. Jr. and Gutzman, Kevin R.C. *Who Killed the Constitution.* Random House (2008). Crown Publishing Group.